My Literary & Moral Meanderings

RUSSIAN & EAST EUROPEAN STUDIES

Jonathan Harris, Editor

University of Pittsburgh Press

My Literary & Moral Meanderings

APOLLON GRIGORYEV

TRANSLATED BY MICHAEL KATZ

with an introduction by Wayne Dowler

Published by the University of Pittsburgh Press, Pittsburgh, Pa., 15260

Manufactured in the United States of America
Printed on acid-free paper
10 9 8 7 6 5 4 3 2 1

ISBN 13: 978-0-8229-4855-1
ISBN 10: 0-8229-4855-9

COVER ART: Background image from *Panorama de Moscou* by Dmitri Stepanovich Indetsev, 1848; illustration of Grigoryev by Alex Wolfe.

COVER DESIGN: Alex Wolfe

Contents

Note on the Translation

This new translation is based on the authoritative and well-annotated Russian text published by Nauka in Leningrad in 1980.

Acknowledgments

I am indebted to the late Ralph Matlaw, an expert on nineteenth-century Russian literature, who was a retired professor at the University of Chicago, and whose translation of Grigoryev's memoir, titled *My Literary and Moral Wanderings*, was published by Dutton Paperbacks in 1962, and is now out of print. Matlaw's version was groundbreaking at the time, but was marred by syntactic literalism and occasional inaccuracies and inconsistencies; furthermore, it contains only four footnotes for a text that demands comprehensive annotation.

I am also deeply grateful to my dear colleague at Middlebury College, Lecturer Emerita Alexandra Baker (aka, Alya) for her careful vetting of my rough draft, and for helping me render Grigoryev's endless sentences into readable English prose.

I am dedicating my own work on this translation to Alya Baker with affection and appreciation for her friendship and her assistance on my translations during the past twenty plus years I've spent at Middlebury.

Introduction

Wayne Dowler

The first installment of *My Literary and Moral Meanderings* appeared in the thick journal *Time* in 1863. Mikhail Dostoevsky, the owner of *Time* and coeditor with his younger brother Fyodor, challenged its author Apollon Alexandrovich Grigoryev to write an autobiography that included his childhood. The childhood autobiography was already an established genre in Russia. Sergei Aksakov, Lev Tolstoy, and Alexander Herzen were predecessors, whom Grigoryev referenced in his own memoir. The censors closed *Time* during the Polish revolt of 1863. In 1864 Dostoevsky opened a successor journal, *Epoch*, and at his urging the installments resumed. *Meanderings* was much more than a memoir. It was an experiment in which Grigoryev examined his childhood through the lens of organic criticism, a literary critical theory that he had painfully worked out over the years. Much more will follow on organic criticism. In essence, it positioned the artist as the intermediary between the unconscious tendencies or currents in a given time and place and their conscious expression in national life. Grigoryev's memoir undertook to uncover the currents prevalent in Russia and from abroad that shaped Russian reality through their revelation in literature and formed, through the filter of the Zamoskvorechye district of Moscow, young Apollon's earliest awakenings.

Readers today might find the primacy ascribed by Grigoryev to art and especially literature in shaping national consciousness surprising. But in an authoritarian state as Russia was and still is, where all the sites of public participation in nation-building are foreclosed and where what it is to be Russian is prescribed from the top down, Grigoryev's effort through organic criticism to unravel the relationship of life to art and art to national consciousness makes sense and even seems necessary. In Russia, writers are often seen as secular prophets.

Although not typical, Grigoryev's career is in many ways illustrative of the lives of the Russian intelligentsia in the mid-nineteenth century. Faced with the demands of state service, censorship, an impecunious and querulous press, rejection, impoverishment, and the challenges of family life in an uncertain environment, many led, as did Grigoryev, disorderly and sometimes tragic existences. A persistent theme in Grigoryev's poetry was struggle, often associated with unrequited love. The poet struggled to submit his ego to the will of fate, to accept the irony of life. Grigoryev was better read than the majority of his contemporaries; he thought deeply about European culture and about Russian national identity and its expressions in art. He exercised a profound influence on Fyodor Dostoevsky, Ivan Turgenev, and other writers of his time. Best known for organic criticism, he also contributed broadly to mid-century Russian cultural life. What follows is an amalgam of biography with an examination of the philosophical sources and evolution of organic criticism, reflecting Grigoryev's own blend in *Meanderings* of autobiography and literary critical theory.

He was born in July 1822. Grandfather Grigoryev had built a small family fortune and achieved hereditary nobility through state service. The Grigoryev family's rural estate, severely damaged during the war of 1812, was partitioned; the remainder produced little revenue but supplied a number of household servants. The family first lived in a rented house in the Zamoskvorechye district of Moscow and from 1830 in a purchased home elsewhere in the district. Apollon's father, Alexander Ivanovich, after a brilliant debut in service with the Senate, was demoted, as a result of his heavy drinking, to a relatively low rank on the Table of Ranks. His son, too, became a binge drinker. The boy's mother was a serf with whom Alexander Ivanovich had fallen in love. His parents blocked the marriage; the couple's illegitimate child was by law registered in the petty townsmen estate, a taxpaying category.

In *Meanderings*, Grigoryev documented his unusual early education far better than any summary could achieve. We commend the reader to his account. As he left childhood, his promise was evident to all. He had studied piano and become an accomplished musician. He had already mastered French and soon acquired German. When his tutor Sergei Ivanovich Lebedev graduated from Moscow University in 1832, the prominent professor of jurisprudence I. D. Belyayev undertook to prepare Apollon for university entrance. The impediment of his illegitimate birth, which threatened him with military service, was overcome when a Moscow magistrate discharged him from the petty townsmen estate on condition that he complete a university degree. In 1838 he entered the faculty of law at Moscow University. The star professors in the faculty were adherents of the philosopher G. W. F. Hegel. With characteristic impetuosity, Grigoryev became an ardent Hegelian and hosted a student group that met in his bedroom to discuss their hero.

The faculty of law prescribed a broad education. Literary theory, theology, Russian and universal history, and other courses were mandated. Grigoryev's professors included the historian T. I. Granovsky, who was among the Westernizers in Russia's cultural debates, but also Mikhail P. Pogodin and S. P. Shevyryov, professors of history and literature, respectively. They were proponents of the "official nationality" that rooted

Russian nationality in autocracy, Orthodoxy, and nationality. Grigoryev formed a lifelong attachment to Pogodin, who became his mentor and surrogate father. In Grigoryev the rector of the university S. G. Stroganov and faculty members identified their most promising student—so promising that in the repressive atmosphere in Russia under Nicholas I, Stroganov feared for his student's safety and advised "il faut vous effacer."

In the early 1840s Moscow University was engulfed in the two great "waves," as Grigoryev called them, of idealism and romanticism. Apollon's early infatuation with Hegel soon passed. The greatest influences on his intellectual formation were J. G. von Herder and F. W. J. von Schelling. Herder stressed the autonomy of national cultures, all of which were of enduring value and contributed equally to the totality of humanity. He argued that the ideal is accessible only through local and immediate experience. In his *Naturphilosophie*, Schelling posited the identity of mind and nature, which gave humans direct access to knowledge of the workings of nature. In 1799 in his *System of Transcendental Idealism*, he positioned the artist as the medium through which nature entered human consciousness. The universe revealed itself through the creative production of the artist.

Grigoryev completed his degree in 1843 and worked briefly in the university library before serving as secretary of the university council. The expectations of the professoriate that he would join its ranks were to be disappointed. Romantic and sensuous, Grigoryev frequently fell in love, though his feelings were often undeclared. The parents of one of his beloveds married her off to another suitor. His next passion was Antonina Fyodorovna Korsh. Antonina and her sister Lidiya were disciples of George Sand and her doctrine of the "liberation of the heart." Before he had the courage to declare his love, Antonina became engaged to K. D. Kavelin, a law student who later became one of Russia's few liberal thinkers. Humiliated by his chronic failures in love, Apollon fled to Saint Petersburg.

After securing a leave of absence from Moscow University, he took a service position in the capital. He began to drink. Often absent from work, he soon sought and received permission to retire from state service on the grounds of ill health. In Saint Petersburg he continued to write poetry and published a small booklet of his verses. In addition he became a contributor to a Saint Petersburg thick journal where he learned the skills of a journal editor. He familiarized himself with the ideas of the so-called utopian socialists, especially those of Charles Fourier, but later declared that he had never been a socialist. As his reputation grew he began to publish articles in a number of the capital's journals and newspapers about the relationship between literature and nationality and his belief that the ideal was accessible only through the particular. He also introduced a theory of types, later a pillar of organic criticism. He identified two fundamental types in Russian history: the predatory type traced back to the Varangians, who, according to the *Primary Chronicle*, founded the Russian state at the invitation of the humble type, the Slavs who had invited the Varangians to rule over them.

By the end of 1846 Grigoryev had fallen into debt. Life in the capital had become too oppressive for him. His parents and friends in Moscow campaigned for his return home. In January 1847 he was back in the city of his birth. Soon, he married Lidiya Korsh, the sister of his beloved Antonina. Children followed in 1849, 1850, and 1852. To support his family, Grigoryev resumed state service and took a teaching position in the Orphans' Institute. When it was transformed into a Cadet Corps, in which he was not certified to teach, he and his students transferred to the Moscow Foundling Home where he was contracted to teach his charges until they graduated. To supplement his income he also became senior teacher of law at the First Moscow Gymnasium in March 1851. By then he had attained the rank of titular counselor; his distinguished service there led to a further promotion in 1856 to collegiate assessor. While Grigoryev was falling platonically and silently in love with one of his sixteen-year-old pupils, he learned that his wife was having an affair. He related the circumstances of his discovery to Ivan Turgenev, who re-created them in *A Nest of Gentlefolk* (1859) in which Lavretsky discovers his wife's infidelity.

Grigoryev had long wished to collaborate in the *Muscovite*. His mentor Pogodin had established the journal in 1841 with the assistance of his university colleague Shevyryov. Under the banner of "autocracy, Orthodoxy, and nationality," the *Muscovite* was conservative and nationalistic. Pogodin shared the belief of the Slavophiles that Western Europe was in decline; he saw Russia as unique politically and culturally; its destiny lay in the renovation of the Christian world. Unlike the Slavophiles, who pointed to the discontinuity of Russian history since the reforms of Peter the Great, Pogodin believed that the Petrine reforms were fundamental to Russia's mission of creating a universal synthesis of East and West.

Falling readership at the end of the 1840s compelled Pogodin to recruit fresh forces to revitalize the journal. A chance meeting in a tavern of the struggling dramatist Alexander Ostrovsky and Tertiy Filippov, an aspiring philosopher with a golden singing voice, sparked an alliance that was soon joined by Evgenii Edel'son, a literary critic, and two poets, Boris Almazov and Lev Mey. Filippov, a colleague of Grigoryev at the First Moscow Gymnasium, introduced Apollon to the group. Grigoryev begged to be included in their number. Pogodin reluctantly ceded editorial control of the belles lettres and literary criticism sections of the *Muscovite* to these promising "young editors."

Grigoryev recalled that the three principles underlying the philosophy of the young editors were: art or the primacy of artistic creativity over all the activities of mind and its inseparability from nationality; democratism or the essential unity of all Russians in a national ideal; and immediacy or the rejection of theory and the direct perception of the concrete historical experience of a people expressed consciously by artists. The young editors took particular interest in music, both folk and classical, and sought to promote a national drama and theater. They shared Pogodin's belief in the exhaustion of Western Europe and held that Russia had absorbed the best of European forms and values thanks to the Petrine reforms. In the plays of Ostrovsky about merchant life they saw the clearest revelation of Russian nationality. They argued that as a group the merchants were culturally close to all the social strata of the nation and foreshadowed their future unity.

Grigoryev began to contribute to the *Muscovite* in 1851. His return to Moscow from the capital coincided roughly with the publication of *Selected Passages from Correspondence with Friends* by Nikolai Gogol. The work was widely viewed as a betrayal of Gogol's previous writings. The critic Vissarion Belinsky responded with a furious outburst accusing Gogol of treason against the progressive ideals of social and political transformation, championed in his play *The Government Inspector* and his novel *Dead Souls*, in favor of passive Christian humility. Grigoryev argued instead that Gogol had been consistent throughout his life in advocating the correction of human error and abuse through Christian example. He attributed Belinsky's failure to understand Gogol to Hegelian historicism. Historicism, he believed, viewed reality through the lens of an abstract preconception and rejected all that did not conform to it. According to Grigoryev, "natural school" critics assumed a critical and negative attitude to Russian reality and valued literature primarily as a weapon for the realization of preconceived social and political goals. He condemned the utilitarian approach to literature and that of art for art's sake, which denied art's social value. In Grigoryev's view, every work of literature reflected the time and place in which it was written; the life it depicted, however, was subject to the judgment of universal aesthetic and moral laws inscribed in the human soul. From Gogol, Grigoryev concluded that the salient feature of Russian nationality was Christian humility.

Grigoryev believed that his colleague, the playwright Alexander Ostrovsky, represented a "new word" after Gogol in the growth of national consciousness. Theater was Grigoryev's new passion; he established himself as Russia's leading, if most controversial, theater critic. In his view, between 1847 and 1855 Ostrovsky had created a truly Russian national theater. The way of life the playwright depicted, his attitude to that way of life, the characters who expressed it, and the tones of the language the characters used spoke to all Russians and awoke in them a new sense of the national being. The plays created new types that no one had previously known to have existed. Like Gogol before him, Ostrovsky captured evolving national life directly and immediately. Grigoryev's cult of Ostrovsky earned him a great deal of ridicule in rival journals. Ostrovsky, himself, began to chafe at Grigoryev's excesses, which some observers saw as an impediment to the dramatist's wider public acceptance.

By 1855 the future of the *Muscovite* was in doubt. Pogodin refused to pay his closest contributors adequately. He frequently interfered in the sections of the journal that the "young editors" were supposed to control. Negotiations between Pogodin and the "young editors" to transfer full editorial control to the latter broke down. Tensions also arose among the young editors themselves. Ostrovsky offended Grigoryev by altering some passages in his articles without consultation. Some close collaborators withdrew from editorial decision making, leaving Grigoryev, whom Pogodin did not trust, in charge. Plans to attract new backers for the journal failed, as did a proposal for Grigoryev's ownership. In 1857 the *Muscovite* ceased publication. Although able to place some articles in other journals, Grigoryev's negotiations with both Slavophile and Westernizer publications for a permanent post failed. It is indicative of Grigoryev's positioning in the intellectual debate between Slavophiles and Westernizers that both sides seriously considered taking him on. His determined independence, however, resulted in acceptance from neither camp.

By the middle of 1856 Grigoryev was bankrupt. In August he fell ill with smallpox. He recovered but compounded his troubles with bouts of heavy drinking. He had long wanted to travel in the West. In 1857 the government granted his application to leave state service to enable him to assume the post of tutor to the fifteen-year-old Prince Ivan Trubetskoy, the scion of one of Russia's most prominent families, resident in Florence. Young Ivan's father had studied with Pogodin, who secured the position for Grigoryev. He seized the chance to pocket a secure and handsome salary and escape from his dissolute life in Moscow. On his way to Florence, he made stops in Berlin, Prague, Vienna, and Venice, where, enchanted by the view, he stepped across the pavement from his hotel and fell into the Grand Canal. On arrival in Florence he got on well with his student, whom he found to be intelligent and sensitive, but whose artistic side was undermined, he complained, by the selfishness of the young aristocrat.

He took great pleasure in the monuments of art that he had seen on his journey and in Florence. "Salvation," he confided in a letter to Pogodin "lies only in the Uffizi and Pitti." But soon he began to fret about the routine of life in the Villa San Pancrazio. He reread Schelling's *Philosophy of Mythology*. It confirmed his opposition to what opponents of the Enlightenment called "scientific universalism." They argued that the theory of progress with its universalizing thrust posed a threat to the variety of human life, to the uniqueness of nations and regions, to the originality of national cultures, to social differentiation, and to individuality and personality. Like many among the Russian intelligentsia, Grigoryev drew a sharp distinction between the greatness of the European past and its present acquisitive pettiness and bourgeois conformity. The theory of progress and a uniform humanity endowed with rights were ideals located in the future. For Grigoryev and other critics of the Enlightenment like Herzen, meaning in life should be sought only in the present and not in a theoretical future. Imbued with the humility of Orthodoxy, said Grigoryev, Russians believed in the human soul, not in the abstract idea of humanity. He added that the official Russian Orthodox Church stood against true morality.

A plan to send Ivan Trubetskoy to attend Moscow University in the following year with Grigoryev as his tutor fell through on the objection of Ivan's mother that universities only corrupt youth. Then, on a visit with the family to Paris and driven by disturbing news from home, Grigoryev went on one of his periodic binges. Although Prince Trubetskoy wanted him to return to Florence with them, Grigoryev knew that the Princess would not forgive him. He returned to Russia in October 1858.

Against the odds, his return was met with professional success. He settled in Saint Petersburg and published a number of articles on a range of subjects. His creative outburst caught the attention of Fyodor Dostoevsky, who planned, when he was freed from exile, to join his brother Mikhail in the publication of *Time.* The elder Dostoevsky had already attracted a number of young contributors to the journal who were anxious to draw Grigoryev into the enterprise. Two articles particularly intrigued them. The first was a review of the early volumes of Sergei Solovyov's *History of Russia.* Since the publication of Nikolai Karamzin's *History of the Russian State* in the first quarter of the nineteenth century, historians had engaged in repudiating the extreme Moscow-dominated centralization that Karamzin had imposed on the nation's history. In that regard, Solovyov's study failed, Grigoryev argued; it was written without any knowledge of the regions and their many differences. Grigoryev's attack on centralization in the writing of Russian history and literature became central to the program of *Time.*

The second article marked the culmination of Grigoryev's formulation of organic criticism. In a review of Russian literature since Alexander Pushkin's death, he positioned Pushkin as the progenitor of the whole of contemporary Russian literature. Previously critical of Belinsky, he found that in his early writings Belinsky had correctly understood the centrality of Pushkin in Russian literature. Neither the utilitarian critics among the nihilists nor the art-for-art's-sake critical school understood the moral and social significance of Pushkin. Grigoryev's idea of types, both humble and predatory, now came to the fore. He argued that in his character Belkin, Pushkin had brought the humble type into literature and therefore into conscious life. With Aleko in the poem "The Gypsies," he had embodied the predatory type. All the character types in literature since Pushkin, he maintained, flowed from the characters drawn from Russian national life that Pushkin had brought to consciousness through his art. Grigoryev noted Pushkin's universality, by which he meant his ability to absorb not only Russian but also West European thought and values. Karamzin, Belinsky, and Herzen had similarly remarked on the ability of Russians to assimilate European ways and ideas.

Literary success, however, did little to relieve the struggles of Grigoryev's personal life. Payments for his articles did not provide a living. His efforts to revive the *Muscovite* or to take over the editorship of the *Russian Word* failed. Again he had formed an association with a woman. Early in 1859, on one of his prowls through the brothels of the capital, he met Mariya Fyodorovna Dubrovskaya. She had fled to Saint Petersburg from the provinces to escape an abusive father and had chosen prostitution to escape poverty. Grigoryev plucked her from the brothel and set her up in separate quarters in his boardinghouse. At first the relationship was platonic. Grigoryev wished to divorce his wife who remained in Moscow, but strict divorce laws made it virtually impossible. Poverty pursued him; he became a familiar in the local debtors' prison where, removed from daily struggles, he wrote some of his finest articles.

Grigoryev joined *Time* late in 1860 and published his first article in it in January 1861. *Time* was the voice of a new tendency in the Russian cultural milieu that became known as the native soil movement (*pochvennichestvo*). In some ways it was a continuation of what the "young editors" had begun. But it was also a response to the nihilism of Nikolai Chernyshevsky, Nikolai Dobrolyubov, and others in the radical press. Dostoevsky saw the task of *Time* as the analysis of the nature of the present moment of Russian social life. The men of the soil believed in the primacy of life over abstraction or theory. They rejected the centralizing and leveling inherent in rationalist thought and believed that humankind could attain its full potential only through the flowering of every nationality. Each would make its unique contribution to the whole. In Russia, they supported regionalism over centralization. They shared with the Slavophiles the conviction that unlike the West, where social division and conflict were the norm, the social classes of Russia enjoyed peaceful relations. They therefore rejected the central tenet of Slavophilism—that Peter's westernizing reforms had divided the nation irretrievably between an educated elite and the people. Instead, the reforms were a manifestation of the Russian capacity for universality and a necessary aspect of the country's cultural development. They acknowledged the gulf between the educated and the masses but positioned it as a stage in a larger process of the creation of an organic whole consisting of elements from all the social strata of the nation.

The program of *Time* incorporated most of the ideas that Grigoryev had formulated over the years. Dostoevsky made use of much of Grigoryev's critical vocabulary and imagery and shared most of his views on art and society, Slavophilism and Westernism, Russian history, and nationality. There were some differences between them. Dostoevsky positioned *Time* among the progressive journals and sought to find grounds for reconciliation with the nihilists. Grigoryev remained highly critical of the leading nihilists. Later, Grigoryev opposed Dostoevsky's emerging messianic universalism, the belief that Russia was destined to reconcile the differences between East and West and renovate a dying Europe. The task of nations was to be themselves; no nation had a universal role to play or any prescribed destination. On his side, Dostoevsky judged Grigoryev to be both difficult and impractical.

Grigoryev's most important contribution to *Time* was a series of articles comprising a history of the intellectual and spiritual life of Russia since the eighteenth century. Here a new element entered his thinking. Previously, he had stressed the primacy and ultimate victory of the humble over the predatory type in Russia's spiritual development. He now recognized that the humble type could produce only stagnation. The predatory type, he had come to believe, was an essential contributor to the full development of personality and society. Although he criticized the leading nihilists, the logic of organic criticism required him to recognize the necessity of nihilism in Russia's development. The materialist and rationalist moment of consciousness embodied in the nihilist Bazarov in Turgenev's *Fathers and Children* was a legitimate part of the process of human consciousness. But it, too, was fleeting; art would ultimately rescue the world from "final reason."

Grigoryev's dedication to regionalism was on full display in *Time*. He admired the work of Afanasy Shchapov, the historian of Siberia who underlined the area's uniqueness and advocated its autonomy. Unlike most Russians of the time, Grigoryev recognized the existence of a distinct Ukrainian nationality expressed in the early writings in Ukrainian of Gogol. In an obituary of Taras Shevchenko, Grigoryev compared the beauty of expression of the Ukrainian poet to that of Pushkin and the Polish poet Adam Mickiewicz. Later, in the face of the nationalistic reaction against the Polish uprising, he courageously asserted the cultural rights of nationalities. In particular, he defended Ukraine's right to its own language and literature, against official Russian policy.

Grigoryev also weighed in on the "woman question" that had occupied the intelligentsia since the 1840s. He argued that men and woman differed but were complementary. Conventional morality and social attitudes had, however, distorted their relations. Education encouraged women's dependence on men, and marriage was debased. The tyranny of men over women destroyed their essential complementarity. Like John Stuart Mill, he advocated changes to social attitudes and women's education to restore it.

Grigoryev should have found a home in *Time.* Its program incorporated almost all his cherished ideas. His reluctance to work under restraints imposed by others, however, reasserted itself after a few months. The Dostoevsky brothers began to edit his articles and asked him to publish them anonymously. He refused. There were other drivers of his alienation. In the progressive intellectual and cultural environment of the early 1860s, Grigoryev felt superfluous. He called himself the last of the romantics and signed some of his articles as an "unnecessary man." His solution as before was to flee. Ten years earlier he had taken a course that qualified him to teach in military schools. He decided to take up a teaching post in the frontier city of Orenburg. Mariya accompanied him. Their new life began well, but quickly soured when Grigoryev's advanced views about education became known. Soon, news that the couple was not married spread. First Mariya left for Saint Petersburg, and Apollon followed, after an extended bout of drinking. From there, he successfully petitioned once again for relief from service on medical grounds.

During the last two years of his life, Grigoryev contributed articles to *Time* and its successor *Epoch.* In them, he applied his organic criticism to analyze the works of Turgenev, Ivan Goncharov, Ostrovsky, Nikolai Nekrasov, and the young Lev Tolstoy, among others. He also assumed the editorship of a new journal named the *Anchor: Messenger of Social Life and Literature, Theatre, Music, and the Arts.* The journal concentrated on Grigoryev's hopes for the growth of a national Russian theater and national music, especially opera. He was a passionate supporter of Alexander Serov whose opera *Judith*, he believed, provided a foundation for the future of Russian opera. The *Anchor* was popular in theater circles but found little favor among the general public.

His personal life worsened as well. His mentor Pogodin ended relations with him after the debacle with the Trubetskoy family. His mother had died, and his relations with his father soured over money matters. In spring 1863 his father also died.

Grigoryev had briefly reunited with Mariya, but she soon abandoned him. The young philosopher Konstantin Leontyev tracked Grigoryev down to a squalid room in a poor district of the capital. The months before his death were punctuated by drunken binges, periods of recovery, and spells in debtors' prison. Shortly after release from prison in September 1864, he died in his room of a stroke after a heated argument with a publisher. He had many mourners, but neither Mariya nor Lidiya was among them. The former learned of his death only after the funeral and begged to know where he was buried; her fate is unknown. The latter died some years afterward in a fire started when she fell asleep while smoking in bed.

Grigoryev's most controversial contribution to *Epoch* was *My Literary and Moral Meanderings.* In it he applied the principles of organic criticism to the cultural milieu in which his early consciousness was formed. Organic criticism valued literary works not for their aesthetic merits as in art for art's sake, not for their location in a larger body of literature as in historical criticism, not for their contribution to preconceived goals as in utilitarian criticism, but for their role in bringing the social and moral tendencies or currents inherent in a particular time and place into consciousness primarily through the creation of literary types drawn from life. In *Meanderings*, the characters are both real and representatives of those types. Even the worst literary outpourings were of value. Grigoryev drew heavily on the foreign and native writings, both bad and good, on which he had eavesdropped late into the night, to portray the era of his childhood. The atmosphere of the restoration in Europe following the exile of Napoleon and in Russia in the somber aftermath of the Decembrist Revolt and the hanging of its most prominent leaders cast long shadows on the life and literature of the time.

Meanderings adopted a conversational form. It was highly discursive, as were most of Grigoryev's articles. His critics believed his complex writing was the product of muddled thinking. In fact, Grigoryev was a remarkably clear thinker. The problem was that organic criticism was antipathetic to the linearity of expository writing. He resorted to a breathless, kaleidoscopic text that jumped rapidly from author to author and title to title in order to imitate the chaotic but organic wholeness of the era.

Grigoryev was aware of Alexander Herzen's reflections on his childhood in *My Past and Thoughts*. The two men had much in common. Both were born out of wedlock, baptized in the same church, and raised in Moscow. Both evoked time and place and sought to use their personal experiences to illuminate the historical forces that shaped their youthful lives. Both gained their early experience of the common people from household servants. They also differed. Herzen's story unfolded against a backdrop of great events: the seizure and burning of Moscow in 1812, the Decembrist Revolt, his father's powerful friends, sightings of tsars, swearing of oaths, sacrifices made, a story with heroic dimensions. Grigoryev's story unfolded in a cloistered home in the little world of the modest Zamoskvorechye district of the city. It was a tale of human weakness, flawed character, failure, compromise, and stifled sensuality. Herzen celebrated the education of personality through social conflict. Grigoryev pointed to the inner contradictions of personality that resisted the lessons of the social environment. Guided by his belief that the ideal was accessible only through the currents and tendencies present in specific times and places, in *Meanderings*, Grigoryev painted a portrait of his inner self, the self-conscious product of those currents and tendencies received through the medium of literature.

Michael Katz has provided an admirable translation with comprehensive annotation of this difficult text. It brings to life for English readers one of Russia's most important and all-too-human thinkers about Russian nationality, a subject again topical in the Russia of today.

My Literary & Moral Meanderings

APOLLON GRIGORYEV

Dedicated to Mikhail Mikhailovich Dostoevsky

Grigoryev dedicated his work to Mikhail Mikhailovich Dostoevsky, a Russian short story writer, publisher, literary critic, and the beloved elder brother of Fyodor Dostoevsky.

Author's Introduction

You challenged me, my dear friend, to write my "literary reminiscences." Although in general, it's dangerous to listen to one's friends because they often get carried away, this time I'll ignore the guidelines of official caution. Besides, to tell the truth, I've paid little attention to them during my entire life.

I'm forty years old, and during at least thirty of them I've lived under the influence of literature. I say, "at least," because I began to live, that is, to think and dream, very early; since then, as soon as I began to think and dream, I did so under one or another literary influence.

As you know, I've been frequently reproached, perhaps justifiably, for the use of various strange terms that I introduced into literary criticism. By the way, there's the word "tendency [*veyanie*]" which, for example, I frequently use instead of the usual word "influence [*vliyanie*]."[1] Something mystical has been

1. The word "*vliyanie*" conveys the meaning of trend or current, something wafting through the air.

associated with these words, although it would be more appropriate to explain them as pantheistic.

So many literary eras have rushed both above and before me, even rushed by within me personally, leaving certain layers, or, rather, traces on my soul that each one regards me from behind a distant past with its own separate organic whole, and has its own special color and aroma for me.

Ihr nach euch wieder, schwankende Gestalten.[2]

At times I invoke them and I hear and sense the miracle of the spirit of their time.

There it is, the era of thin, gray little issues of the *Telegraph* and the *Telescope*, read greedily by young people in the 1830s who surrounded my childhood—an era when Pushkin's verses were still being mumbled and the aroma could be sensed in the air everywhere, even in the dense gardens of the surprisingly typical Zamoskvorechye—an era of unconscious and uniform enthusiasms, into which young people were transported along with those eternal songs and with *Ammalat-bek.*[3] It was an era over which the dark cloud of its predecessor hangs, in which are reflected some of the sinister gloomy tendencies of that period and Polezhayev's tragic fate.[4] In spite of the unconscious and indifferent enthusiasms, of unrestrained ecstasy over poetry, and of some sort of ordinary faith in literature, there remains something gloomy and disturbing in the air. People's souls are

2. "You've come again, you shifting shades" (Ger.). This is the first line of Goethe's *Faust* (1829).

3. The *Telegraph* and the *Telescope* were popular Russian journals of the period. Zamoskvorechye is a mercantile district of Moscow south of the Moscow River. The era referred to is the late 1820s, after the Decembrist Revolt. *Ammalat-Bek* (1832) was the best-known and most popular of the poet Alexander Bestuzhev-Marlinsky's "southern" works. Bestuzhev-Marlinsky (1797–1837) was a popular Russian writer and Decembrist. He was exiled to the Caucasus where he perished in a battle.

4. Alexander Polezhayev was a controversial Russian poet, best known for his satirical poem *Sashka*, which in 1826 resulted in his being demoted to the Russian Army in the Caucasus.

filled with that gloomy, disturbing, and ominous feeling: Polezhayev's verse, Mochalov's acting, and Varlaam's songs reflect the mood of the time.[5] And then the colossal novel by Hugo appears and it turns young people's heads; then Nadezhdin in his *Telescope* constantly feeds the romantic fever with his translations of youthful, feverish works by Dumas, Sue, and Janin.[6]

The air is clearing. . . . A powerful voice rings out, simultaneously legitimizing and spurring on the aspirations and vague speculations of the era—the voice of that great fighter, Vissarion Belinsky.[7] In his *Literary Musings*, as in every work of genius, he combines everything that had transpired into a single whole and at the same time he casts his nets into the future.

Another era is wafting through the air.

My own personal childhood had ended a long time ago. I didn't have a boyhood and, strictly speaking, I didn't have a youth either. My youth, genuine youth began very late, and it was something between boyhood and youth. The head works like a steam engine, rushes impulsively into ravines and abysses, while the heart lives only dreamily, in a bookish, pretend life. It was as if I wasn't living this life, but various literary images were living in me. On the threshold of that era were written the words: "Moscow University after the reform of 1836," the university of Redkin, Krylov, Moroshkin, Kryukov, the university of mysterious Hegelianism, with its ponderous forms and striving, force bursting invincibly ahead—the university of Granovsky.[8]

5. Pavel Mochalov (1800–1848), a popular tragic actor of Russian Romanticism, was known for his performances in melodrama, tragedy, and Shakespeare. Varlaam is a character in Modest Mussorgsky's opera *Boris Godunov* (1872).

6. Victor Hugo, *Notre-Dame de Paris* (1831). Alexandre Dumas (1824–1895), Eugene Sue (1804–1857), and Jules Janin (1804–1874) were three influential nineteenth-century French novelists .

7. Vissarion Belinsky (1811–1848) was the foremost Russian literary critic of the early nineteenth century. His *Literary Musings* was published in 1834.

8. Timofey Granovsky (1813–1855) was the founder of medieval studies in Russia and a professor at Moscow University.

"A change came over the spirit of my Dream."[9]

By the will of the fates or, better to say, by an invincible thirst for life, I was transported into another world. That was the world of Gogol's Petersburg, the city in the era of its illusory originality, to an era when there even existed a special Petersburg literature. . . . In this new world a streak of completely fantastic life even flashed; over my moral nature passed a strange mystical tendency—but, on the other hand, I found with it's rather rotten smell and its rather dirty color, the world of Panayev's "Rot," the world of the Pestsovs, Mezhakovs, and other dark figures, the world of Alexandriya in the full bloom of its development with Grigoryev's vaudevilles and the still wandering Nekrasov-Perepelsky, with a special armchair for a certain wealthy young merchant and with a talented actress who forced you to forget this terribly vulgar world.[10]

And then—it's Moscow once again. The dreamy life is over. Genuine youth begins with a search for real life, with harsh lessons and experiences. New meetings, new people, people who are not bookish at all, or very little, people who "retain" in themselves and in others everything put on, everything warmed up, and carry in their souls a faith in the nation and nationality unpretentiously and naively to the point of unconsciousness. Everything "national," even local, that surrounded my upbringing, everything that I almost managed to stifle in myself for a time, after giving myself up to the powerful tendencies of science and literature—rises up in the soul with unexpected strength and grows, grows to a fanatic exclusive measure, to the point of intolerance and propaganda. . . . Five years of a new school of life.

And then another break.

9. An inaccurate quotation from Byron's lyric, "Dream" (1816).

10. Ivan Panayev (1812–1862), a writer and journalist, wrote a tale titled "Rot." The talented actress referred to is Vera Samoilova, a well-known actress of the Alexandrinsky Theatre in Petersburg.

Western life unfolds before my own eyes with the wonders of its great past and once again it teases, rouses, and attracts. But that lively confrontation did not destroy belief in oneself, in the national. It merely softened the fanaticism of that faith.

Such is the intellectual and moral process.

I don't know if I possess sufficient talent to outline these various eras, to communicate them with their color and aroma. If only sincerity were required for this—sincerity would be total, so far as intellectual and moral life are concerned.

One thing I know for sure: I am exclusively the son of my era and my literary confessions can have a certain historical interest.

—September 12, 1862

Part One

Moscow and the Beginning of the 1830s in Literature

My Infancy, Childhood, and Adolescence

I

First General Impressions

If you've visited and lived in Moscow and you don't know such parts of it as, for example, Zamoskvorechye and Taganka—then you don't know its most characteristic qualities. Just as the Travestere in ancient Rome, perhaps not without reason, boasts that in it are preserved old Roman types,[1] Zamoskvorechye and Taganka can boast a similar preeminence before other parts of the enormous city-village, the monstrously fantastical and at the same time the splendidly developed and extensive growth called Moscow. From the nucleus of all ancient Russian cities, from the Kremlin, or the fortress, there grew first a white, trading town; then came an earthen city, and various suburbs began to spread beyond the Moscow River. The old-fashioned way of life escaped from the influence of the administrative regime and was unfalteringly concentrated in them. Deprived of the possibility of developing independently, it sank into stagnation on its own account. The general law

1. Colorful Trastevere is an area of Rome that adheres to its age-old, lower-class roots.

of our history is the withdrawal of the zemstvo system of life from the external norm into the solitary and stubborn seclusion of sectarians.[2] This was also repeated in Moscow, that is, in the development of its way of life.

Have you ever visited Zamoskvorechye? It has frequently been depicted satirically. Who hasn't described it that way? Truly only a lazy man! But up until now, no one, not even Ostrovsky,[3] has treated its poetic aspects. But these aspects exist—well, just as a first example, the external aspects, and obvious ones. In the first place, it's a good thing that the further you enter it, the more Zamoskvorechye drowns in green gardens in front of you; in the second place, its streets and lanes branch off so freely that they must have grown on their own and were not laid out. . . . You will be sure to get lost, but you will do so with pleasure. . . .[4]

Come walk with me, for example, from the Large Stone Bridge, straight, straight ahead, as the crow flies. We pass the so-called Marsh. . . . Yes! The main thing is, imagine that we're walking there late one evening. We pass the Marsh with the official building of the Wine Exchange; so far there's nothing special here. As a matter of fact, there is, except one would have to turn into Bersenevka or Solodovka, but we won't go there. We reach the Small Stone Bridge, the only old-fashioned bridge to somehow survive the zeal of our reformer-builders, which reminds me of bridges in Italian towns, for instance, those in Pisa. Before us are the three main arteries of the Zamoskvorechye, that is, strictly speaking, there are only two: the Large Polyanka and the Yakimanka; the third one between them is not that large. These two arteries lead us to the so-called gates: one, the right artery, to the Kaluga Gate; the other, the left, leads

2. The elective district council in Russia from 1864 to 1917.

3. Alexander Ostrovsky (1823–1886) was a Russian playwright, regarded as the greatest dramatist of the Russian realistic period. He described the less well-heeled classes in his dramas.

4. Ellipses in this translation are part of the author's original text unless otherwise noted.

to the Serpukhovsky Gate. But the gates aren't what matters, all the more so because once upon a time they marked the end of the city's arteries, but they no longer exist, and the city has grown broader, beyond these gates.

I could go with you along the right artery; moreover, I could escort you at its festive, triumphant moment on the clear morning of August 19, when large crowds of people are moving in a religious procession to the Donskoy Monastery, and all the sidewalks are filled with the population of the right bank of the Zamoskvorechye, dressed in celebratory fashion; the air quivers with the sound of bells of old churches, and everything rejoices for some reason, happy to be alive, whether with the combination of the most trivial matters or with something larger, I don't know, but in common, even though vague; yet something affects the entire crowd for the moment. And truly, I'm an incorrigible, inveterate Muscovite—this moment is splendid. Some kind of general feeling is shared by the whole assorted crowd; it seizes you, too, a civilized man, if only you don't stubbornly resolve not to submit to the impression, and if you stubbornly struggle against this form.

But you and I won't go along this artery: instead we'll go along the left one, where, as soon as you set out, you'll encounter a large Italian house designed in fine Italian architectural style. We proceed for a while along this artery, and nothing special strikes you. One house after another, most of them made of stone and of good quality, each clearly intended for a single family; there are spikes on top, the houses are guarded by watchdogs on chains at night; your nerves shudder from the sudden, ferocious barking of a dog, who rushes the fence in a fit of jealousy and vehemence. Among the stone houses from time to time there are small, low wooden houses, but they're somehow neglected, uninviting looking, as if aware that they're out of place on this fine, wide, large street.

Further on: pause for a moment in front of the low, dark-red church of Gregory Neocaesaria with its onion domes. It's not really lacking an original physiognomy, though *something* was obviously being mulled over in the architect's head when it was being built; but in Italy this *something* would have been built on the grand scale in marble; yet here the poor fellow executed it on a small scale and made of brick. Nevertheless *something* emerged, whereas nothing comes of the large number of churches built after the reign of Peter the Great. However, I was mistaken when I said that the architect would have built something on a colossal scale in Italy. In Pisa I saw the church of Santa Maria Della Spina, a tiny little church, but so heavily adorned and, at the same time, so strictly styled, that it seemed grandiose.

Now we've reached the Polyansky Market; meanwhile it's become very dark. Here and there lights have been lit in houses, not only in taverns.

We won't stop in front of the Church of the Assumption in Kazachye. Although it was at one time an old church because its name alludes to the presence of Cossacks, the zeal of its wealthy parishioners had long since renovated it and now, like the old cathedral in Tver, it has taken on a general, official character. Let's turn left. In front of us stretch lovely, cozy houses with very long fences; the houses are by and large one story, with mezzanines. There's light coming from the windows, and there are boiling samovars on little tables; everything inside looks so domestic and welcoming that if you weren't a family man or a visitor, a certain feeling of envy would begin to discomfort you. An Arcadia created in your own imagination attracts and teases you, although, perhaps, it doesn't really exist in fact.[5]

Continuing to walk with you to the left, I lead you into the most original part of Zamoskvorechye, in the direction of the Ordynsky and Tatar suburbs, and at last to the neighborhood of Bolvanovka, called that because here, according to local legend, our princes met the Mongol tax collectors and bowed down to the Tatar idols.

5. A mythical region of simple peace and quiet.

Right here on the Bolvanovka began my somewhat-conscious childhood, that is, a childhood that had and retained some sort of meaning. I wasn't born here; I was born on Tverskaya; I can remember myself from the time I was three or even two years old, but that was my infancy. Zamoskvorechye nourished and pampered me.

I'm intentionally emphasizing this geographical fact of my personal life. Perhaps I'm obligated to the strength of my first impressions for the outcome of the intellectual and moral processes that occurred within me, my turn to the passionate worship of the zemstvo national life.

I intend to write not an autobiography, but a history of my impressions; I take myself as the object, as a complete stranger; I view myself as one of the sons of a particular era, and therefore, only that which characterizes this era in general way should be included in my reminiscences; my personal details will enter the picture only insofar as they serve to portray the era.

That task is even easier for me, if you like, because I have long had the accursed custom of reasoning, more than describing.

And so, first of all, I have to pause on one personal trait of my early development, which seems to me to be very characteristic of our entire generation. The process of reflection began unusually early in me, before I was five years old, namely from the time when, by the will of fate, my family moved to a remote and strange corner of the world called Zamoskvorechye. I recall very clearly, as if it were only yesterday, that at the age of five, I already had an Arcadia for which I pined, a lost Arcadia, which, in comparison to the present, seemed to me to be somehow sad and gray, precisely gray. For me this Arcadia was life near the Tver Gates, in the house of the Kozins. Why this life seemed to me to be suffused with some sort of light, why even at my young age I would always pass that house with a trembling heart, even though its ownership had long since passed to a new owner, and why I often visited that house under the pretense of looking for a new apartment, trying to recall the nooks where I played in my childhood, why, I say, this Arcadia pursued me, is a very complicated matter. On the one hand, there's the general characteristic of my era, and on the other, if you like, it was something physiological, hereditary, and domestic.

Our entire family had its lost Arcadia, one of a rich life with our late grandfather before the French incursion, which destroyed his two houses on the Dmitrovka; and in particular, one of my aunts, who was an extremely dreamy and exalted woman, filled with this "golden age"; and besides, they represented two different eras.

I was born in 1822. I can recall myself and my unconscious impressions at the age of three. The social catastrophe that occurred at this time, a catastrophe some of whose victims my father knew personally from his stay at the University School for Noblemen, had a major impact on my childlike feelings.[6]

Adults consider children somehow stupid and never suspect that at least something of what they see and hear impacts their souls and their imaginations. For example, I remember as if in a dream, but I really do remember, how they carried the body of Tsar Alexander I back, and what strange fear prevailed in the air at that time. . . .[7]

No one and nothing can convince me that ideas aren't something organic, carried by, and wafting in the air, substantial, something due to the order of succession. . . .

That which drifted at the time over everything, that which greeted me on my entrance into the world, I can, of course, never express as well as did the highly gifted and passionate Musset in his *Confessions d'un enfant du siècle.*[8] I will remind you of this remarkable passage, with which I will conclude this sketch of

6. "Social catastrophe" refers to the rout of the Decembrist Revolt.

7. Aleksandr I died in Taganrog in 1825 and his body was transported by train back to Moscow.

8. *Confession of a Child of the Century* (1836) (Fr.) is a novel written by Alfred de Musset (1810–1857), the French poet and dramatist.

the threshold of my impressions: "During the wars of the Empire, at that time, when husbands and brothers were serving in Germany, anxious mothers produced a fervent generation, pale and nervous. Conceived between battles, educated in schools amid the sounds of war, thousands of children regarded each other gloomily, while testing their weak muscles. From time to time their bloodstained fathers would appear, lift them to the chests covered in gold, then lower them to the ground, and remount their horses."[9]

But the war ended: Caesar died on a distant island.

Then an anxious youth sat himself on the ruins of the old world. All these children were drops of fiery blood that had intoxicated the earth: they were born amid battles. They held the whole world in their heads; they looked at the earth, the sky, the streets, and the roads—everything was deserted, and only the sound of parish church bells sounded in the distance.

Three elements shared the life that offered itself to these children: behind them a past, destroyed forever; ahead of them, the dawn of an immense horizon, the first rays of the future, and between these two worlds, something like the ocean, which separates the Old World from America; I don't know, something indefinite and unsteady, a sea that was troubled and threatened shipwreck, at times crossed by some distant white sail or a ship at a slow speed; the present century, our century, in a word, and one that separates the past from the future, and that is neither one thing nor the other, and that resembles both one and the other, and at every step one wonders: Am I walking over seeds or more ashes?

Only the present was left for them, the spirit of the age, the angel of dusk, who is neither night nor day; they found him seated on a sack of bones, wrapped in a cloak of egotism and shivering from the cold. The torment of death crept into their

9. This passage is Grigoryev's own version, since Musset's *Confession* was still not available in translation at the time.

souls at the sight of this vision, half-mummy and half-dust; they approached it like the traveler in Strasbourg who's shown the corpse of the daughter of the old count Saarwerden,[10] embalmed in her casket wearing her wedding dress. That childish skeleton is terrible, because on her thin pale fingers she still wears a wedding ring, while her head disintegrates into dust amid the flowers.

"Oh, peoples of the future!" the poet concludes his introduction. "When on some hot summer's day you're bending over your plow in the green field of your fatherland, when under the rays of the bright, pure sun, the earth, a bounteous mother, will smile in her morning attire on the peasant farmer; when, wiping from your tranquil brow the sacred perspiration, you'll rest your eye on the endless horizon and remember us, who'll no longer be living—you'll tell yourself that we paid dearly for your future peace; pity us more than all of your forebears. They had a great deal of sorrow, which rendered them worthy of compassion; and we lacked that which consoled them.

10. Strasbourg is a county located in Lorraine, France.

II

The World of Superstitions

Literary works that are serious and grasp life in all its types are a good thing. Moreover, while they are good in and of themselves, positively good—they also have a negative use: after grasping certain well-known types, and immortalizing them artistically and boldly, they eliminate any desire to repeat them.

Thus, for example, if Aksakov's *Family Chronicle* did not exist,[1] I would become unavoidably more involved in relating details about my grandfather, a person I never saw because he died a year before my birth; but thanks to family stories, he was known to me inside out, and he played a not insignificant role in the history of my moral impressions.

Now one only has to agree about the general type of stout men of the former period, depicted boldly and simple-heartedly by the late Aksakov, and only note the differences and distinctions, and there emerges a portrait that, if not drawn by me, can easily be outlined by the reader.

1. Sergei Aksakov (1791–1859) was an important nineteenth-century author, known for his semi-autobiographical works, including *A Family Chronicle* (1856). The hero of the work is the patriarch Stepan Bagrov.

In his general traits, my grandfather was astonishingly like Aksakov's old man Bagrov; his day, at the time when he could live in peace, differed very little from Bagrov's day, judging by family tales. I recall that he didn't even own a hazel stick, but he had his own Tanaichenok, even his own Kalmucks—that I remember very well.[2] The difference between him and Stepan Bagrov was only that he, being the same kind of substantial person, was placed in different life conditions. He wasn't born a landowner, but he became one, only at the end of his busy and difficult life. He arrived in Moscow from the northeast wearing a short sheepskin coat, made his way by the sweat of his brow, and for his era, carved his way rather successfully. He did so, of course, by service and because he was by nature intelligent and energetic. He had one more remarkable characteristic—his thirst for education. He was extremely well read in religious books, and would even argue on occasion with bishops; he left behind a rather large library, a practical one, which we, his heirs, for some reason valued very little. . . .

By the way, he had another strange trait, one that also seemed to be pervasive in our development—it's that we all are one half Peter the Great and the other half Oblomov.[3] At times we are prepared to destroy violently all traces of the entire past, carried away by enthusiasm for the first thing we meet; and later we almost burst into tears thinking about what we ignored and destroyed. I was already almost eleven years old when they brought boxes with grandfather's old books from the country to Moscow. That was already the era of various pseudo-historical novels, which I delighted in reading unceasingly, everything from *Yury Miloslavsky* to *David Igorevich*, and other works unknown today from Lazhechnikov's *Novik* to Rafail Zotov's

2. Tanaichenok is a peasant lad in Aksakov's *A Family Chronicle*. Kalmucks are a Buddhist Mongol people living in Kalmyk territory in Russia.

3. That is, men of action (Peter the Great) versus lazybones (Oblomov). Oblomov is the "hero" of Ivan Goncharov's novel by the same name (1859).

Leonid.[4] Grandfather's old books had a strange effect on me in their yellowed leather bindings; they were gloomy tomes, staid, sometimes in large folio, printed in old Slavic characters, like the spiritual anthology of prayer, the *Dobrotolyubye*,[5] or in small octavo, in eighteenth-century script; original works like Emin's, and translated works by John Bunyan and Johann Arndt; there were tiny half-worn editions, so rare today, of satirical journals such as *Both This and That*, and *All Sorts of Things.* As if it were yesterday, I remember how I regarded them with some carelessness, how I—I'd been given the right to arrange the library—didn't want to honor them by placing them on the same shelf with all the *Leonids*, *Coaching Inns*, *Dmitry the Pretenders*,[6] and other such nonsense, with which, under the influence of the age, I filled the bookcase, separating them only from the works by Karamzin, which I was brought up to respect irrationally.[7] I remember that I even trampled them underfoot in indignation, and still, consumed with a thirst for reading, glanced into them, those old books, and even perused the satirical periodicals of Novikov's era (I could never manage to read "Roslad" and other odes, along with Knyazhnin's and Nikolev's works);[8] I was obliged to these old books for my familiarity with the life and

4. *Yury Miloslavsky* was written by Mikhail Zagoskin (1829); *David Igorevich* by Rudnevsky (1834); *Novik* by Ivan Lazhechnikov in 1831; and *Leonid* by Rafail Zotov in 1840. All four works are historical novels describing various epochs in Russian history.
5. *Dobrotolyubye* was published in 1793–1794. Fyodor Emin (1735–1770) was one of the first Russian novelists, best known for his *The Letters of Ernest and Doravra* (1766). John Bunyan (1628–1688) was the author of the Christian allegory *The Pilgrim's Progress* (1678); Johann Arndt (1555–1621) was a German Lutheran theologian who wrote books of devotional Christianity.
6. *The Coaching Inn* was written by Aleksey Stepanov in 1835; and *Dmitry the Pretender* by Faddei Bulgarin in 1830.
7. Nikolai Karamzin (1766–1826) was the most important late eighteenth-century Russian writer of poetry and short stories.
8. "Roslad" is most likely a reference to Mikhail Kheraskov's heroic ode *The Rossiada* (1779). Yakov Knyazhnin (1740 or 1742–1791) was an outstanding Russian tragic author. Nikolai Nikolev (1758–1815) was a Russian poet and dramatist.

thoughts of our nearest predecessors. In my later years I regretted that lost library, stolen by drunken lackeys and consumed by hungry mice. But alas! As we do everywhere and in everything, we come to appreciate our heritage too late.

My grandfather was even acquainted with Novikov: the legend in the family was preserved that he'd been frightened after Novikov's arrest and even burned many books that had been given to him as gifts by Nikolai Ivanovich. I can't say for sure whether my grandfather was a Mason or not. Our relatives didn't know anything about that. A certain person who was a member of that society, and who had, as I will relate in due course, a great influence on me and on my development, used to say that he was indeed a Mason.

My grandfather and the world that once thrived around him, a world of abundance and even excess, carriages with four fine horses, a world of terrible Bagrov-like despotism, piety, domestic quarrels—this was an Arcadia for my aunt, but not at all for my father, a good-natured and intelligent man, but not at all excitable.

When my grandmothers and my aunts came from the village to visit us, I fell completely under the influence of my eldest aunt; I will speak about her more than once: she was a rather typical figure. She had a passionate and talented nature and never married due to her terrible pride; she concentrated on memories of the past. Even her tone was constantly exalted, but it was only in my later years that this tone began to seem comic to me. As a child I surrendered to her stories, her dreams of a fantastic golden age, even her unrealistic, but persistent, hopes for the inevitable return of a golden age for our family.

There was even a time when . . . I promised to be absolutely truthful in everything that related to my spiritual development . . . a period not of my first youth, when, under the influence of mystical ideas, I believed in some enigmatic connection between my own soul and that of my late grandfather, in some sort of metempsychosis, not really that, but a harmony of souls.

Frequently, while returning at night from Sokolniki, always choosing the longest way home because I loved to wander in Moscow at night, when I reached the Church of Nikolai the Martyr on Basmanaya Street, I would pause before the old house on the corner, my grandfather's first refuge when he arrived in Moscow to make his fortune. Sitting down on the chapel porch, I would wait there for half an hour to see if my old grandfather would appear to solve the large number of problems that were troubling my soul. The prey runs to meet the hunter. A person inclined to mysticism frequently encounters facts that are inconsequential to other people, but which draw him personally into that strange abyss. Twice in my life, and always prior to various crises, my grandfather appeared in my dreams. The phenomenon is quite explicable psychically, but it nurtures the soul's inclination to enter the mysterious world.

Superstitions and legends encircled my childhood, just as they do the childhood of any young nobleman, whether of great or limited means, surrounded by a large or small number of servants, and at times left entirely under their supervision. The servants, and this had been so from time immemorial, in spite of the fact that my father lived well enough, were all from the country, and I spent my time in the world that Goncharov had described so masterfully in "Oblomov's Dream."[9] When relatives would arrive from the country, several members of their large staff of servants would accompany them; they added fire to my superstitious, or better to say, my fantastic inclinations with new tales of mysterious goats butting heads at midnight on the little bridge to the village of Malakhov, or about the treasure in the Kirikov forest—one of the principal foundations of my aunt's hope for the return of Arcadia, or about the magician-peasant who was buried at the crossroads. Add to all this the fact that my old great uncle, my grandmother's brother, who later, when

9. The most famous chapter in Goncharov's novel, one in which the child Oblomov lives in a romantic dream world.

I was ten years old, lived with me in the attic of our house, spent his time reading sacred books and praying, and who even died while praying; but every evening until then he would tell me stories about corpses and witches with absolute conviction; then add to this my great aunt, who came from the country with my grandmother, a woman who was the embodiment of simplicity and kindness, able to cure the entire district with home remedies, who never lied, and yet who, according to her own tales, witnessed all sorts of things in her life.

This world of superstitions acted upon my outrageously nervous nature in such a way that, at the age of fourteen, having absorbed the tales of Hoffmann in addition,[10] I would literally suffer at night in my attic, where I slept next to Ivan, or Vanyushka, who was a year younger than I was. I listened to the striking of the clock feverishly and uneasily; it would hiss and croak furiously, and I would always only fall asleep after midnight, when in the predawn hours, the cock would crow.

All of that passed in time, my nerves grew coarser, but you know I would pay dearly to experience that sweetly pacifying, cloyingly tormenting mood, that sensitivity to the fantastic, that proximity to another, strange world, just as nervously as I did then. . . . After all, the fantastic remains in the human soul forever; therefore, since I believe only in the soul, it must to a certain extent be all right.

10. E. T. A. Hoffmann (1776–1822) was a German novelist and short-story writer whose enormously popular tales became the basis of neo-Gothic literature in the early nineteenth century.

III

The Servants

But it wasn't only superstition that developed my early attitude to the common people. One great writer in his reminiscences had already uttered a good word in favor of so-called servants and one's attitudes to them, describing his own youth.[1] There is also no lack of bad features in this tainted transplant of national life, bad features caused by slavery, not by transplantation; many bad features, of course, also affected me, and that occurred at the wrong time. Sexual instincts were aroused early in me; since they were always merely aroused and not satisfied, they provided employment for my unbridled fantasy; I also learned early on all the intricacies of forceful Russian speech; I heard my fill of tales about farmhands and their well-known masters—and I really must consider the coachman, Vasily as my mentor, almost on a par with my first teacher. . . .

But there was a good side, almost a sacred side to my getting to know the common people, even with its tainted elements. It goes

1. Alexander Herzen (1812–1870) published his brilliant memoirs, *My Past and Thoughts*, in 1870.

without saying that my father and mother acted unconsciously in failing to separate me from intimate relations with the servants; in any case, this does great honor to their simple and well-meaning view, the more so since in them, as in our entire family, the feeling of gentry ambition was terribly developed in all other aspects of life. In this, however, everything proceeded as of yore according to the established order. One must also say, to their credit, that my parents' own relations with the servants were in large part humane, that is, as humane as it was possible under the conditions of serfdom. Our servants ate well, worked little, and drank, both men and even older women, drank to a great extent. Once my father decided against purchasing a house that was for sale at an auction simply because there was a tavern next to it. Then, according to my mother's *fundamental* objection, it would've been necessary to extract Vasily and the elder Ivan from it all the time, and my old nurse, Praskovya, as well. By the way, I said that the treatment of the servants by my parents was humane for the *most part*, and I said that for good reason. My mother's sense of strict justice was developed to the highest degree, but from the age of nine, I can't recall her being healthy. I don't know what the illness was, but it continued until her death. Doctor Ivan Alekseich Voskresensky, well known in the Taganka and Zamoskvorechye, kept treating her, but for more than twenty years the illness devoured her, and for several days each month my poor mother ceased being a regular human being. Even her outward appearance would be altered: her eyes, clever and clear during normal times, would become cloudy and wild, yellow spots would emerge on her tender face, a malicious smile would appear on her skinny lips, and she would forget every feeling of justice. . . . Completely lacking in education, reading haltingly, even though she was endowed from birth with wonderful good sense and even an aesthetic sense—she could sing very well by ear—my poor mother was totally altered by some terrible illness. During a surge or attack of her disease, the bright, decent sides of her personality would disappear, qualities that were good in moderation, as for example, economic solicitude and thrift, were taken to the extreme: instead of her spiritual qualities, there appeared only egotism, a person gifted by fate but deprived of all the means of personal development. There were moments—alas! as life proceeded, the rarer they occurred—when she seemed to become brighter and younger. The splendid and refined features of her face would clear, without ever losing a certain severity (though more like a sad seriousness); her movements would lose their harshness and become pliable; her voice, painfully strained, would sound like a gentle contralto. Oh, how I loved her during those infrequent moments! Where did she suddenly get such feminine tact in conversations with strangers, such an absence of shrugs and grimaces, of plucking and primping herself, which distinguished her so sharply from all the other ladies of our circle, ladies who for the most part resembled Khorkov's mother in Ostrovsky's play, *The Poor Bride.*[2]

On the other hand, my father, a good-natured man with a clear mind, whom my late grandfather, an energetic and stout man, called by the name of Israel, partially sarcastically; even frightened in part from childhood, he would sometimes, though rarely, repeat in life Grandfather Bagrov's outbursts.[3] And it wasn't because at the time he was driven beyond the limits of human patience by the shenanigans of the servants. If that had been the case, there would have been enough reason to be driven to such a state daily. No, this was something physiological, a tribute to something innate, something completely insane and ferocious, something whose attacks I felt in myself, of course, for different reasons, to which I also surrendered like a wild beast. . . . Over time these attacks of innate madness in him became less and less frequent. In both his appearance and character

2. *The Poor Bride* was written in 1851 by the dramatist Alexander Ostrovsky (1823–1886).

3. For "the name of Israel," see *Genesis* 32: 24–28. For Grandfather Bagrov, see Aksakov's *A Family Chronicle.*

he resembled his mother, my grandmother, whom I knew only as an old woman, and who always seemed to me to be imperturbably calm, tranquil, profound, but never pompous; her speech was intelligent and she felt endless tender and restless solicitude about her poor daughters, my old aunts, with the memory of her Ivan Grigorich; he was stern and not always equable, with clear traces on his character of the influence of this substantial person, traces obvious in her sound religious ideas, in her steadfast belief in justice. . . . Yes! From many signs I can conclude that my grandfather was far from being an ordinary man. During the time he was in government service, probably like everyone else, he accepted if not bribes, then voluntary extortion, but such were the ideas of his surrounding milieu; aside from these ideas, he had a strong sense of right and honor, and, according to everyone who knew him, including distant relations and strangers, he had an invincible Old Testament faith in the God of Israel, a God of truth; there was also in him a sacred pride that forced him not to hold his tongue wherever he was and no matter with whom . . . before the members of the higher orders of clergy, with whom he loved to associate, and before secular powers with whom he was fated to come into conflict.

But once again I've been carried away by my favorite image of childhood, this ideal with which for a long time I associated my clever and good-natured, but not at all typical, father; in no way did I see that he had an entirely different nature; I loved him instinctively, but I didn't respect his own personal good sides.

My father's generic outbursts and my mother's monthly attacks of illness destroyed the ordinary lack of discipline in our lives, but they developed in me a feeling of compassion to the point of a disease. I howled hysterically when they punished the coachman Vasily or his wife, my former nanny, for drunkenness, or the servant Ivan for his carousals with the lads. . . . I always acted as the intermediary in such cases, and my father, even in his fits of rage, appreciated that role of mine as a result of his own good nature. It was a good thing that he liked it, but it was useless that he showed me that he did. It developed in me some sort of early theatricality in my feelings, an early capacity for suspecting my own sensitivity. . . . I remember—I was around nine years old—having first sobbed instinctively, I looked in the mirror to make sure I appeared sufficiently distraught, before going in to my father to beg for Ivan or Vasily, who'd been sent to the police.

In any case, I was on very intimate terms with the servants. They kept no secrets from me, because they knew that I wouldn't betray them. When I was fourteen or fifteen I even used to lock the doors after vespers when Ivan slipped away to a rendezvous with one of his mistresses, and I would unlock them for him when it was time for matins; when I was already a student, several times I carried the coachman Vasily home in my arms late at night, even unlocking the gates quietly. . . .

And they loved me, of course, loved me in their own way—they loved me until the time later when their interests began to clash with my own. It goes without saying that there was no reason to blame them for selfish love. The fault wasn't theirs; it was due to the system of serfdom, which corrupted the noble Russian nature. One old nurse (she also served as our cook for a long time, until they *bought a new cook*) loved me instinctively, whole-heartedly—she even died with the wish to cast her eye on me, although I was in Petersburg at the time of her death—and that was, I think, because she was a free woman from the town of Arzamas; after becoming a widow, she'd married the drunken serf coachman Vasily, whom she loved passionately. . . .

Still, I owe a great deal to you, the disorderly, depraved, selfish servants, for my development. . . . There aren't any folk songs, or very few of them that are foreign to me: imprinted on a child's ear, they sounded like old friends in my late youth; forgotten for a time, neglected, even scorned, just like grandfather's old books, they rose up again in the soul, in all their spontaneous beauty. . . . I played all the folk games with our servants in the large courtyard, stickball, and even leap-frog, when my mother and father had gone visiting and didn't take me along: all the fairytales of the folk epic about the fox and a wolf, a fox and the rooster, the life of the rooster, the tomcat and the fox in the same house—I heard them all in the autumn twilight from the country lass Marina, who was brought from her village to entertain me as I lay there in an old lair in the barn, wrapped up in a fur coat.

Sometimes peasants would come from grandmother's village. They were a source of even more wonderful tales—as I spent most of my time in the kitchen with the peasants. I knew them all by their stories, many of them personally; warned in advance, they didn't stand on ceremony with me and didn't hold back. . . . I loved them terribly and, at funerals, saying farewell to the respected peasants, like the village elder Grigory, I even mentioned them in my childhood prayers, right after my relatives and those closest to me. . . .

IV

The Neighborhood

One must say that the neighborhood was such that it could leave indelible traces on one's soul.

I began the history of my impressions with a general picture of Zamoskvorechye, risking, obviously consciously risking, being torn to pieces by our various denunciatory periodicals. I've already said it seems that Zamoskvorechye is not only a special world, but a combination of diverse special worlds, each one bearing its own distinct, typical features.

Let's stand together, readers who have already visited Moscow, on the Kremlin heights, from which the southeastern, southern, and southwestern parts of the city form an enormous semicircle before you. If I hadn't brought you here from the very beginning, to the Kremlin heights, then I'm sorry to say that it was to avoid a routine way of doing it. The view of Moscow from the Kremlin heights is almost as commonplace as the view from the Vorobyov Hills. Even now I pause here with you on this point because I need to do so. . . .

The panorama is huge and colorful; it strikes you by its colors and its size, nevertheless, there are certain outstanding points on which you can fix your gaze. . . . On the left it settles in the far distance on two large monastery bell towers: Novospassky and Simonov. . . . The old monasteries are something like precious stones in the crown delineating the enormous budding city, or, if this comparison seems mannered—something like a metal hoop. . . . The point isn't in the color of the comparison, but in its essence; its essence, if you regard it without prejudice, will be true: the old layers of the city are pulled together by a hoop with bracelets—namely, monasteries within the city limits—the former Alekseyev monastery, which I still remember, where now the Cathedral of Christ the Saviour stands; in the place vacated by the Novinsky, Nikitsky, Petrovsky, and Nativity-Andronyevsky monasteries; the expanding suburbs are also girded by a hoop of a horizontal line along which legitimate points attracting one's gaze are also monasteries: Novospassky, Simonov, Donskoy, and Devichy.

I called your attention to the distant points of the horizon because I am attracted to one of these points, using a supple pre-Petrine expression of our forebears to describe one part of Moscow or another with a special character. Within the city circle, the monasteries have lost their significance as points of attraction, although previously they probably possessed it: after all, on the hoop of Kitay-gorod there are also nameplates—Znamensky and Bogoyavlensky Monasteries, and so on. In Zamoskvorechye and Taganka, which "pulls" half to the Andronyevsky, and half to the New Church of the Saviour, the typical character of the monasteries is more intact, naturally. The special character, special color, and smell of life in southeastern Zamoskvorechye "pulls" toward the Simonov Monastery, and in the southern and southwestern part, toward the Donskoy Monastery. . . .

Walking with you into the heart of the Zamoskvorechye, I've pointed out two of its three main arteries, ending at gates that no longer exist, but I didn't mention the third, the huge, southwestern artery, Pyatnitskaya Street, named after the church dedicated to the mythical folk saint Pyatnitskaya-Praskovya.

But it's not that church which strikes and arrests your eyes from the Kremlin heights, when you gradually turn your gaze from the southeast, toward the south, but the splendid church of the Roman pope Clement with its five cupolas. You will pause before it: walking along Pyatnitskaya Street, it will strike you by the severity and grandeur of its style, even the harmony of its parts. . . . But it stands out from the multitude of various ornamented churches and bell towers, also original and unusually picturesque from afar, which characterize Zamoskvorechye in particular. . . . Proceeding through its winding streets, moving further and further into its depths, perhaps you will come upon the more original style of the older, squat, ornamented churches with onion domes, but from afar, it is Clement that undoubtedly reigns over all of them. The mostly merchant life, along Pyatnitskaya Street and to its right, becomes concentrated in its stone houses, courtyards with fences, frequently made of stone, too; to the left, the merchants' life mixes with that of the small tradesmen, minor officials, and even, perhaps, lower gentry. Walking to the left along Pyatnitskaya, you even make it to the Hook, that astonishing corner of the world, where one of the dramas by Alexander Ostrovsky takes place, the most impossible from the humanitarian point of view, and at the same time, one of the most realistic, *Hangover at Someone Else's Feast*,[1] in which the landlady of an honest teacher accepts a receipt from Andryusha Bruskov for marriage to her lodger's daughter, and Kit Kitych pays for that receipt because he doesn't know what the good-for-nothings might do; in secret he's afraid of them, although he puts on airs before the drunken good-for-nothing Sakhar Sakharych. . . . Here between the Hook and the Moscow River are two lives: the zemstvo inhabitants of villages and the good-for-nothings who live side by side and who weave together like plants, although they don't ever mix and certainly don't merge.

1. Written by Ostrovsky in 1855.

You see, I took you to the Kremlin heights merely for you to distinguish the two parts of Zamoskvorechye. My childhood transpired in the first, the southeastern part; my adolescence and early youth in the other, the southwestern part. . . .

The life surrounding me in my childhood was half that of gentry, half that of "good-for-nothings" because my father was a civil servant and served in the kind of office where the average civil-servant level of life didn't enter; there, clerks caroused, did their business, and chicanery ruled. . . . The life of the good-for-nothings came into contact in many ways with the life of the land, and in particular, in that part of the world that lay between the commissariat, the Hook, and Pyatnitskaya.

I can see it now—the gloomy and dilapidated house with an attic, painted in faded yellow, with the inevitable alabaster decorations on its façade, and some sort of animal statues on its mournful old gates—a house with gentry pretensions, where my conscious childhood began. Two such similar houses stood side by side, and at one time both belonged to the same gentry family, not very well known, but average. . . . The inhabitants of the house into which we moved from Tverskaya, were the female remnants of this once well-to-do family: the widow-lady and her two unmarried daughters. The owner of the other house, the widow's nephew, lived somewhere in the country, and that house stood empty for a long time, except for a female ward of his who lived in mysterious confinement in the attic. The strangest rumors circulated about this attic, about the ward, and about the owner of this vacant house himself, who was rumored to be a libertine and a Freemason.

Both houses looked out on the enclosure of the Spaso-Bolvanovskaya Church, which was distinguished only by its name; they stood like some gloomy scroungers, neglected or neglecting themselves from their grief, in line with other well-built merchants' houses, with high gates and fences. Only a stone house belonging to the nobility, and significantly higher nobility, with half-crumbled columns at the end of the lane, nodded sympathetically to them.

Whether it was the gloominess of these houses with their pretentious, noble aspirations, which acted on my impressionable imagination, or it was that my soul at birth was fated to experience a double Arcadia, that is, an inherited one and an imaginary one, but all during our stay there, which lasted some four years until the purchase of another house in the southern part of Zamoskvorechye, I related to this house and the life within it with repulsion, and even with hatred, and I cherished in my childhood dreams the Arcadia of the Tver gates with its large stone house, filled with lodgers of various nationalities, with the noise and racket of children playing in the large courtyard, with memories of the owner, Ignaty Ivanych's gray horses, which he often invited me to see in their clean, bright stable; and the smartly dressed coachman Dementy, who frequently gave me rides from the Tver gates to the place where the Triumphal gates now stand, probably because he liked my younger nanny's light brown hair and rosy cheeks; across the large square with the gates of the Strastny Monastery before our eyes, with the Lord's Passion depicted on them, which my older nanny would visit with me, and explain the images in the same apocryphal-legendary style, as she did the legend of the "Virgin's dream."

Perhaps many things—my mother's illness, which began at that time, and Lebedev's ill-fated Latin grammar book,[2] which I had just begun to study and which I still can't regard without a certain droll feeling of hostility, and the even more accursed arithmetic textbook, with which I could never be reconciled, whether it was by Memorsky, as at first, or Allay, Bill, Puissan, or later Boudreau—many things, I repeat, perhaps cast gloomy darkness over me and my existence, and I related with hostility to life on Bolvanovka.

But the past has a strange power, especially over us members of the former generation. The further I became distanced from

2. Vasily Lebedev's popular Latin grammar was first published in 1762 in Petersburg.

those years, the brighter and brighter they became in my memory. Often when strolling around Moscow at night, in my later years I ventured deep into the left side of Zamoskvorechye, but—alas!—there were no traces left of the past. The well-built merchants' houses survived, but the columns had been removed from the stone house, it had been whitewashed, and given a respectable staid appearance under its new owners; in place of the ambitious gentry houses at the end of the lane, were built new, clean merchants' houses. The church fence itself, which once wound in a crooked line, moved back somewhat, and now stood at attention in order of size. . . .

It's clear why, in addition to the general rule of idealizing the past the farther one gets from it, life on the Spaso-Bolvanovka seemed to me more and more luminous.

Attached to the old house there used to be a garden with a dilapidated fence, which went as far as the Hook, and in the evenings I would watch through holes in the fence the gatherings and fistfights that went on, and how a gang of boys would start a fight; the further it went, the more it would involve the grownups. Oh! How my heart beat then, I so wanted to join that crowd of boys who started the whole thing, me, son of a gentry family, who was protected as if fragile, only rarely allowed (thank God it occurred at all!) to play games with the servants! On major holidays, workers from the factory would come to dance, and I sympathized passionately with our servants who were restricted to the courtyard, and who smacked their lips like a cat, regarding the free life howling freely around them.

V

Last Impressions of Childhood

Yes! I was brought up on tenterhooks; life around me provided only impressions; it teased me, and therefore my daydreaming became even stronger and stronger. At times I was even overcome by an unnatural anguish, especially on long autumn and winter evenings. I was literally immersed in toys, and they bored me.

I was about seven years old when my family began seriously considering finding me a tutor, naturally according to their means, and according to the general custom, as inexpensive as possible. Up to then, my mother had been teaching me the letters, but somehow I never went further than a-b-c; in general, I was incredibly lazy until the age of twelve.

At last they began to look for a teacher for real; but first of all, following the well-known Russian custom of putting the cart before the horse, they bought, for whatever reason, a pointer for the letters. The pointer was made of bone and was very handsome: I broke it within a day, as I had broken all my other toys. I recall it as if it were now: one autumn evening, after the candles had been lit, I was sitting on a rug in the hall surrounded by toys, listening to stories told by the younger nanny, all about grandmother's village; I was trying to figure out what Ivan, who was sitting next to me on the rug, was doing with his dolls, showing them to Lukeriya, and why she was swearing and then laughing—when the teacher, who was a student wearing his uniform with a sword and a brisk walk, came into the living room where my father was. "The teacher, the teacher," said my nanny, and looked at him with curiosity. "A dashing fellow!" added Ivan, and once again began showing her something mysterious.

I started to howl. . . .

I was appeased, with difficulty, by stories about my future bride and her golden carriage, in which I would travel to be married; meanwhile, after a quarter of an hour, the doors to the living room opened and my father, escorting the student, pointed me out to him, then called me over and added, "So you'll begin on Tuesday and good luck to you!"

Tuesday was the saint's day of Cosmas and Damian the Generous,[1] the day on which studies usually begin by custom.

But it seems that customs were fated to surround me, but not be carried out fully. The day of the protectors of learning began. I was seated with the a-b-c book and my broken pointer next to the window and was told to wait for the teacher. I remember that I stared at the street mindlessly and sorrowfully for almost an hour without noticing anything, not even thinking or daydreaming of anything out of the ordinary. The hour of eleven struck—the time established for the lesson, but the teacher hadn't appeared. I was taken away. The clock rang twelve o'clock: still no teacher. It was time for dinner; father returned from his office.

The pride of a member of the gentry awoke in him.

Having been a pupil of the former school for the nobility, a schoolmate of both Zhukovsky and Turgenev,[2] in spite of his

1. Cosmas and Damian were third-century Arabian-born twin brothers who embraced Christianity and practiced medicine and surgery without charging a fee. This led them to be known as the holy "unmercenaries."

2. Vasily Zhukovsky (1783–1852), a poet and translator, was Pushkin's most influential predecessor.

lively mind and kind soul, he was filled with a strange kind of disdain for priests, and that was even stranger because in our family we had a large number of clergy in various ranks: from bishops to deacons, and even down to the lower ranks. However, this was the general failure of my father, an elder aunt, and an uncle, that they didn't appreciate interrogations about the degree of kinship with their uncle, the priest Andrey Ivanych, and with other members of the clergy. Besides, my father felt a special antipathy. Talking about his time spent there, he never forgot to recall how they, the sons of nobility, were obligated to attend lectures at the university during their final year, and would quarrel on the staircases with the real students who came from the clergy, who at the time wore some sort of yellow nankeen trousers tucked into their boots, and foolish uniforms with yellow collars.

To tell the truth, even back then, in 1828, the student uniform was not that handsome: dark blue with a reddish-orange collar, it looked somewhat like a policeman's outfit; the university young people hardly ever wore uniforms, preferring to attend even lectures in their civilian clothes.

For my father, from force of habit, the idea of a student merged with that of a priest's son. Besides, ambition produced in him instantly a generic outburst, and when the student appeared that evening, he received him very brusquely and, in spite of his excuses, fired him.

This explains why my studies didn't commence on the day of the venerable Cosmas and Damian.

Once again, my mother began to teach me the alphabet as she had before, and just as before, we didn't progress any further than a-b-c.

Finally, in another autumn at dusk, already in November, my father's young colleague from work, the secretary Dmitry Ilych Kumov arrived with his wife, an attractive and very bright daughter of a priest, much beloved by my mother for her lively and kind nature, and who was often able to dispel my mother's hypochondriacal attacks by her chatter. They announced at tea that their "kinsman," Father Ivan Lebedev, would join them; he was the priest in a little village near Moscow called Perov. He would be accompanied by his son Sergei, a young "seminarian," who had just enrolled in the university, it goes without saying, at the medical school. And sure enough, not more than an hour or so later, Father Ivan arrived wearing a three-cornered hat and a rabbit fur coat; he was a tall, gaunt old man, with a big bald spot that was revealed after he took off his hat. Following him was a young man with a timid step, downcast eyes, and with rosy cheeks, almost a boy, wearing a course woolen overcoat. He was very good-looking at the time, as I recall. . . . I was not even struck—and I can see him before my eyes now—by the particular saccharine sweetness of his face and his soft-as-butter eyes, which I noticed some time afterward.

I didn't even start to howl.

Father Ivan and Dmitry Ilych emptied about four decanters of a vodka infusion of Saint John's wort. My father didn't drink with them, because some ten years ago he'd given up "behaving like a coward, drinking"; but he kept pouring them drinks, was in a good mood, and he somehow predisposed everyone to merriment; and he made fun of Sergei Ivanych—that was the name of my future young tutor. The instructor, hemming and hawing like a seminarian, blushing, hesitated in his answers; to give himself some heft, he turned to me and asked how and what I'd studied up to this point. I recall that I answered him without the least hesitation and cheerfully led him into the living room to show him my large collection of toys. He couldn't conceal his amazement and for some reason blushed deeply when he laid eyes on my younger nanny.

The matter was settled. The next day Sergei Ivanych was to move into our house.

My "studies" were beginning. . . .

Part Two

Childhood

I

A Seminarian of the 1830s

At the present time when, that is, not what you think—I'm talking neither about progress nor about beneficial publicity—at the present time when literature points out one layer of our society after another and presents its diverse types one after another—the type of the seminarian and his milieu emerge from their previous obscurity. But this is a type, which at different times changes its colors, although, of course, it has its own essential character; this type divides into two, just like all fundamental types of our everyday life; and for the time being, literature develops one of its aspects, primarily in the essays of Mr. Pomyalovsky,[1] that of a strong man, who is gaining a special distinction for himself in one or another sphere of life, by this or that method, positive or negative, it really doesn't matter. The choice of a path depends here on the circumstances of time and the conditions of life, although the starting point

1. Nikolai Pomyalovsky (1835–1863) was a Russian novelist. His best-known work, *Seminary Sketches*, gives a fictionalized but accurate account of his years spent in seminaries.

of their activity is always negation. The strong seminarian was raised on negation. *An non spiritus existunt?*[2] is posed to him as a question; if it's asked positively, his answer is, and must be: *nego*;[3] with his repudiation, he wins the prize for negation. If his school were to pose the question in the negative form: *spiritus non existunt*,[4] he would be negating the negation and instead of being a materialist and a nihilist, he would be an idealist, *e sempre bene*,[5] because practically speaking, then only audacious naysayers are correct: they firmly believe the saying that *gutta cavat lapidem*,[6] and they strike accurately at the same place, without paying the least attention to others, without being carried away by anything except for the question posed by them—even becoming intentionally deaf to all refutations of life and thought. Once a well-known point of view has been fitted into their particular scheme, even if that scheme is a *chreia inversa*, an administrative centralization on the French model, such as in Speransky or Phalansterism, as is the case with many of our literary celebrities—what do they care if life cries out from the prosecutor's box at this same *chreia inversa*, or against this same little administrative or social ideal?[7] After all, they kept breaking them at the seminary, and bending them in the academy—why not violate life as well?

Our literature depicts in gloomy and terrible sketches the life and educational circumstances that prepare the practical negators, revealing it unsparingly, to the point of cynicism, flogging mercilessly—and indeed those circumstances hardly deserve any

2. "Do spirits exist?" (Lat.).

3. "I negate" (Lat.).

4. "Spirits do not exist" (Lat.).

5. "Splendid!" (Lat.).

6. "A drop of water hollows out a stone" (Lat.).

7. A *chreia inversa* is a rhetorical figure meaning "short anecdote" (Gk.). Mikhail Speransky (1772–1839) was a noted Russian reformer during the reign of Alexander I. A phalanstery was a self-contained utopian community developed in the early nineteenth century by Charles Fourier. Nikolai Chernyshevsky popularized the idea in Russia.

mercy. Let those who are in pain, cry out from their pain; their cries merely bear witness to the fact that flogging was correct, that it hit upon sensitive spots—but all the same they deserve to be flogged. After all, those circumstances are given to us neither by our native soil nor by our national life; after all, this seminary is imposed on us just as administrative centralization is, only earlier, perhaps immemorially early. . . . There's no need to regret it: it's not our native Oblomovitis; it is guilty only inasmuch as it doesn't let Stolzitis ride piggyback on it.[8]

By all this I wish to say that literature, which at the current time has undertaken the task of revising this layer of our life and its types, is completely correct in its one-sided depiction. In the milieu of life itself, this type appeared vividly only in its negatively practical manifestation, whether this manifestation is the great historical figure Speransky, or in the spheres of life, the blossoming Maksyutka Benevolensky of Ostrovsky. . . .[9] "A paradoxical and absurd juxtaposition!" say the readers. More than paradoxical and absurd, I will add, it's a blasphemous juxtaposition; for Speransky, at least during the first period of his activity, was moved by the loftiest aspirations, whereas Maksyutka Benevolensky smugly pats himself on his topknot in front of a mirror on account of an extremely insignificant circumstance in history, apropos of his marriage, which, by the way, ends his victories in life. But I have intentionally chosen such extreme examples as the historical Speransky and the fictional Benevolensky in order to demonstrate the importance that type of substantial seminarian possesses everywhere, a fearless naysayer and champion of life.

But this type, like every other predominantly Russian type, has another side, and appears in another guise in life. The split personality is perhaps common to all humanity, but with us Russians, it's somehow more obvious.

---

8. The two main characters in Goncharov's novel *Oblomov*: Oblomov is a model of inaction, while Stolz is the opposite.

9. A character in Ostrovsky's play, *The Poor Bride* (1852).

There are, according to the profound saying by George Sand, *des hommes forts*—strong people, and *des hommes grands*—great people.[10] There are also, according to a profound saying by one of the most original and independent thinkers of our age, Ernest Renan, *des pensées étroites*—narrow ideas and *pensées larges*—broad ideas.[11] "Only narrow ideas rule the world," adds Renan, and this is completely justified. . . . If Sand's idea can't be completed the same way, still one can find in it an affinity with Renan's idea. There are broad people; from them either great people or Oblomovs emerge, and there are strong people, firm, substantial people, from whom great figures emerge, and this even happens frequently, but Oblomovs never do. They give themselves up to life and all its tendencies, and good for them if they are geniuses—representatives of the tendencies of life; others conquer life and rule it. Some don't fulfill any sort of premeditated goals, but, depending on the era in which they are created, they either identify with life itself, or their personality is dispersed in life; others manage to attain some goals, those Speranskys or Benevolenskys: this depends on the degree of their strength and talents, and on the era in which they live and act. Our era—I'm turning again from the general situation to the fate of the type about which I began speaking—brought forward many such substantial figures with a negative, theoretical task. That side of the type had already appeared to me personally during my university years, in the form of the powerful and gifted personality of the late Irinarkh Vvedensky,[12] but definitely no earlier.

---

10. An inaccurate reference to George Sand's *Letters of a Traveller* (1836): she contrasts strong people and good people, and asserts that both groups should be called great.

11. Ernest Renan (1823–1892) was a historian of religion; this quotation has not been located in any of his works. He did write: "People are unified more by their narrow thoughts than by their broad thoughts."

12. Irinarkh Vvedensky (1813–1855) was a translator, critic, and classmate of Grigoryev's at Moscow University. He was a radical thinker and predecessor of the intellectuals of the 1860s.

The era in which my studies began and continued right up until my arrival at university under the influence of seminarians, wasn't the same as that whose harbinger was later Vvedensky, and whose true representatives were Dobrolyubov and Pomyalovsky.[13]

Life lives in protest, but the protest in different eras has different points of departure, different themes, different enthusiasms, so to speak. The personalities that surrounded my childhood were also full of protest, but their protest didn't resemble at all that of today. They were all more or less idealists—it's more accurate and more colorful to say—romantics of all sorts and subdivisions, starting with stormy romantics, who wasted their lives with the frenzy of a Russian, and ending with dreamy and sweet romantics; but, in any case, they were people who gave themselves up completely to life, or at least they submitted to it. The particular characteristic of these people was, in the first place, that almost all of them, and in particular the talented ones, were passionate worshippers of the beautiful, as opposed to the theoreticians, naysayers and centralizers; and the other characteristic was that almost none of them, especially the talented ones, ever built any sort of career. Even those among them with the humblest view of life barely managed to enter the professoriate. While the talented ones, who got carried away or overexcited, like one remarkable deacon-singer who finally chose to be defrocked, or they became government officials who drank heavily, not even attaining the goals of Maksyutka Benevolensky, and even less the touching serenity of Akim Akimovich Yusov's conscience.[14]

"What is so good about this type?" the reader will ask, having perhaps noticed in my tone a particular predilection for this type (which is completely justified), and supposing perhaps (which is completely unjustified), that I give this type preference over

13. Nikolai Dobrolyubov (1836–1861) was a radical critic, journalist, and prominent figure in the Russian revolutionary movement.

14. A character in Ostrovsky's drama, *A Profitable Position* (1857).

the one that developed specially in the current era. But now, please note: in the first place, the gifted individuals who perished were still terribly talented, and the mad turmoil of their strength bears witness, no matter what you think, to the richness of nature; while few of those who grew up unharmed and developed along more regular lines, were well-rounded, solid people who engaged in highly productive activity. It's sufficient to point out in this case the late Pyotr Nikolayevich Kudryavtsev, who, after all, is not to be blamed for dying too young.[15] I'm intentionally pointing out this person, about whom there can be no doubts or misunderstandings in either of our camps, and who cannot be relegated to the type of substantial seminarians, although Kudryavtsev belongs to another later layer, to that of my comrades, and not to those who supervised my education. Kudryavtsev was the most talented and harmonious of the seminarian-romantics. Despite these characteristics, at times, comic traits of the sentimental romantic type also shone in him, and one wicked, although friendly epigram expressed these comic traits in the line, "A pedant, stewed in honey. . . ."[16]

But it seems to me that the comic sides of sentimental Romanticism were not united in anyone as clearly as in my young tutor.

Sergei Ivanych was definitely made entirely of heart, and this heart was unusually soft and impressionable. His nervousness was entirely feminine, and I don't understand at all how that young man could possibly have been enrolled in the medical faculty, studying anatomy, and of course, dissecting corpses, and how he managed to complete his course and become a doctor of the first class, even awarded a little star, that is, named as one of the best. Once after accidentally cutting off his thumbnail, he fainted and imagined that he would contract gangrene, about which he'd just heard a lecture; another time a long, involved

15. Pyotr Nikolayevich Kudryavtsev (1816–1858) was a Russian writer, historian, pedagogue, literary critic, philologist, and journalist.

16. The line comes from a satirical poem (1852?) by Ivan Turgenev.

story occurred when they had to remove an abscess from under his arm. With this feminine, or better to say, old woman's softness of his nature, were combined an egotism that was positively cocksure and an astonishing capacity for self-deception. He was lacking real passion; on the other hand, there was a constant unquenchable urge toward passion, and he urged, urged himself beyond measure—in verse, prose, and various love affairs, which began with him somehow as desired, and about which I will report as much as I can recall in the next chapter, because they characterize this entire era. He also possessed a capacity for enthusiasm, and even though in the end it was cheap and didn't lead anywhere, it produced a very good impression on me. However, God only knows whether it was good or bad.

In our family and in our domestic way of life there existed this peculiarity, that everyone who entered it more or less, willingly or not, became its member, and was infected, at least temporarily, with its special aroma, even submitted, though with a grumble and opposition, to what Fet and I termed the domestic "dogma."[17] Later it developed into rough disorder, exclusivity and individuality. It was not a question of whether we had an established order—where isn't there one? No, anti-rational things constantly became more and more legitimate and indisputable in our house, so that later to encroach on the cook Ignaty's right to drunkenness and violence was considered very dangerous. But that happened only later. . . . At first the peculiarity of our domestic life affected other people more gently. The only misfortune was that if a man was a little too soft, he became something on the order of a domestic fool.

And this is why: my father, in spite of his remarkable intelligence and his education, which was sufficient, although superficial, and therefore completely useless to him and to others, was a humorist by nature, and, like a good Russian, a merciless humorist at that. Strictly speaking, there was no reason for

17. Afanasy Fet (1820–1892) was a renowned Russian poet of the period.

him to be merciful. He had no sort of ideal life or morality: his contemporaries, who had frantically sought an ideal, did so at a time when, perhaps, he had already found it in "the gloomy abysses of the earth,"[18] but he belonged to the rational majority. This rational majority of that era left us with a naive, and hence valuable memoir titled *Diary of a Student.*[19] If the reader is not familiar with this remarkably ingenuous book, I advise him to read it. The spirit of our fathers that resulted in Griboyedov's chastisement,[20] breathes in it.

My father laughed, or better to say amused himself in the most good-natured way, over every feeling; he loved to trample on the feelings of anyone in whom he noticed some impressionability, and he had in my tutor a priceless subject for this activity; he fell in love with him every month and tormented him every day. He even experienced some sort of antipathy toward people who were serious in the least, or who didn't take his bait. He exerted great influence on Sergei Ivanovich, even educated him in his own way, never noticing that he himself was lagging behind the education of the era, if he hadn't done so already. Sergei Ivanovich obeyed him in everything: in his amorous adventures and even in his apparel and manners, he played his fool, and could have selected a less outdated guide. But judge for yourself, how could he, a timid seminarian, very susceptible to an education, not obey a man who spoke French and had studied in the school for noblemen? My father even frequently meddled in his relations with his comrades, using his influence to separate him from boisterous people, that is, from

18. A quotation from Alexander Pushkin's poem, "19 October 1827," hinting at the fate of his comrades who were condemned for participating in the Decembrist Revolt of 1825.

19. *Diary of a Student* was written by Stepan Zhikharev (1787–1860), a young Russian nobleman, who described theatrical and literary life first in Moscow and then in Petersburg at the beginning of the nineteenth century.

20. Alexander Griboyedov (1795–1829) was a Russian playwright, poet, and diplomat. His one notable work was the verse comedy *Woe from Wit* (1823).

those who were incapable of submitting to *l'ascendant* (that was one of his favorite words),[21] and "forming his protégés," students who showed a liking for what he considered education.

On the other hand, my father's protégés, and even those who were tolerable to some extent, would come at any time, and had the right to remain even during class hours and, in general, whole days until the strictly established hour. The dogmatic hour, when the entire house had to sleep de jure, and when de facto the maximum amount of debauchery of every sort began, drunkenness and outrage, gradually moved to ten o'clock in the evening, but at that time, it was not yet so. At ten o'clock the day had just finished for strangers. Sergei Ivanych would go from his little room to my parents' bedroom and read to them, often until one o'clock in the morning, and sometimes even until two. But my room was right next to their bedroom, and I could hear everything that was being read by Sergei Ivanych, just as I heard everything that was read by my father, because they took turns reading.

Reading at our house was a truly passionate activity for a number of years. It had a great influence on my own moral development. Whether because of dissoluteness, or lack of belief that books were something serious, they didn't seem to notice that I would sit in the corner at night where, instead of playing with my toys, I would listen to someone reading *The Mysteries of Udolpho*, *The Italian*, and *The Children of the Don River Monastery*, and many other books.[22] And in the last analysis, I am profoundly grateful for the education I received when they paid no attention to my dedicated overhearing. Thank heavens, I never knew any so-called children's books, and if now I hate them intensely, I myself am surprised by my completely unselfish hatred toward

21. Influence (Fr.).

22. *The Mysteries of Udolpho* (1794) by Ann Radcliffe was one of the most popular Gothic novels of the late eighteenth–early nineteenth centuries. Her last work was *The Italian* (1797). The author of *The Children of the Don River Monastery* is unknown.

them. When they were occasionally bought and given to me, it was never demanded that I read them; glutted by all the toys I had, I would cut out pictures from the children's books.

My early studies, in spite of their disgraceful disorderliness, also had a good side, and, perhaps it was precisely the disgraceful disorderliness. Strictly speaking, I studied very little at that time, but I sat at my studies for a long time, a very long time. On whatever I understood easily, of course, I spent no time at all; whatever could be crammed into me, in spite of my laziness, as a result of my rather strong abilities, for example, in Latin, which I began to study at the same time as Russian grammar, was packed into my head as a result of spending whole days in Sergei Ivanych's room perusing Lebedev's awful little grammar book; whatever I showed no ability for, such as mathematics, I didn't cram at all . . . *ma tanto meglio.*[23] Nevertheless, without having gone through the "fire and brimstone" of schools and seminaries, I was still a seminarian by my elementary education, which, I state frankly, I was proud of.

I remember it as if it were yesterday, that little room in the rear of the house, rather dirty, its window facing the courtyard, which had been designated as Sergei Ivanych's quarters, as well as our classroom, with its old furniture, a table with gashes cut into it and ink on it, near the little window, with its torn dark, leather sofa—the home of a million cockroaches, a skull on the shelf, the essential possession of every medical student. . . . How many tears were shed in that room in the mornings over its accursed arithmetic assignments, how merry it was for me beginning at five o'clock and going until ten, when my studies ended and I was a guest among Sergei Ivanych's friends, students of various departments. . . . The memory of it is so cherished, that dirty little room, the long twilights when Sergei Ivanych would sprawl on the tattered sofa and I would curl up next to him in a ball. There was no candle, he would make me stroke his soft,

23. "So much the better" (It.).

somewhat curly hair, and he would fantasize aloud about his love life, or recount stories from Roman history, which he did very well, and the great figures of Brutus and Cincinnatus, Camillus, and Marius would rise before my impressionable imagination like gigantic ghosts. . . . Eternal memory to you, you dirty little room! Eternal memory also to you, my kind tutor, if you've already died; and if you're still alive and sober, may God grant you a long life; but if you were fated to become a drunkard, alas, my reason tells me that judging by the facts of your romantic nature—you must be living in one of those remote towns that the "devil kept trying to find for three years,"[24] where fate sent you as a country doctor.

24. A quotation from one of Aksakov's own lyrics.

II

An Ordinary Day

Yes! I remember you well, you oblong, dirty little room, although you were never called a classroom: you were simply Sergei Ivanych's room. I remember you at all hours of the day, with all your various changes of decoration.

A winter morning barely begins to break through the curtains of my bed, which was constantly fenced in with boards to protect against my friskiness before going to sleep and my restlessness during the night. Around seven o'clock my father would start coughing in the next room—that meant he was awake, but not yet out of bed, because he had the splendid habit, which he maintained until old age, of not rousing the servants until it was time for my studies, even though he himself would usually rise earlier. But now he's up and around, cups are clattering; then I hear the deaf servant Ivan noisily jumping down from the chest in the hall: a moment later the samovar is heating up. I also begin to show signs of life. My younger nanny, because the elder one had already been promoted to cook, helps me on with my shoes (she helped me on with my clothes and my shoes until I reached the age of almost thirteen, when my uncle, about whom I'll have more to say later, shamed me about it). I go in to my father to say good morning, naturally after having said my prayers in Russian and Latin, according to some Latin a-b-c book. Then my father would pour me a very large cup of tea into which he'd put an enormous amount of sugar, which nauseates me now as I recall it, but not then. Usually my father would remain silent until after he'd had his own tea; then he'd begin to tease me about something, if he was in a good mood; next he would send some tea to Sergei Ivanych, ordering that he be fully awakened; then he'd make me enough tea for the entire day, since as a tender gentry child, I was given only tea to drink, just as a calf is fed milk. . . . I would be cheerful or not depending on whether Sergei Ivanych had complained about me the night before; however, this was always a matter of chance and my tutor's mood, which depended more or less on whether he'd been successful in his amorous affairs, because there was always something he could complain about. However, I was not cheerful, not really cheerful, not because I was afraid of my father. I was afraid of his fits of rage, which could fall upon me just as easily and violently as on the coachman Vasily—but he could vent his anger on anyone and that would be the end of it—the next day it wasn't even mentioned; but my mother—my mother would be implacable, and she would eat away at me maliciously all the while she was drinking her tea, and while she was combing my hair with a fine comb, choosing the most terrible and insulting words to wound my pride. . . .

Now my mother gets up as well; I approach her bed, trembling or not, depending on whether or not Sergei Ivanych had complained of my laziness, or whether the landlady's daughters had complained about my inappropriate pranks. I've never been spanked with a birch rod; I've been threatened with it only once because I pasted a piece of paper on the hem of the laundress's skirt with the name of the deaf servant Ivan (who was her lover). At last, the preliminary morning tortures are complete until nine o'clock. I would run like a madman from my moral and tonsorial combing straight into Sergei Ivanych's room.

But there it wasn't any easier for me. Sergei Ivanych was strict and gloomy in the mornings, that is, he would either put on airs of strictness and gloominess, or else he really was sad as a result of some amorous failure. In the latter case—it was real trouble: he would demand that I recite all the exceptions to the third declension, or would give me a difficult problem to solve in arithmetic, or assign too many lines of sacred history to memorize! He would give me the assignment and then go off to the university for about three hours . . . I would sit by myself in the dining room near the window over my book trying to learn it by heart, or not. My mother was arguing with the deaf servant in the next room either because he would always throw a load of firewood on the floor like a "boor," or else he would feed the nightingale with buckwheat groats, which, according to him, would end up in its cage on its own, or she would argue with Lukeriya, whom she constantly badgered for committing sins against virtue, or with my old nurse Praskovya who was summoned on important occasions from the kitchen—my mother, in a word, engaging in domestic chores, strictly making sure that I stayed working on my lessons both before and after coffee. And I would sit there. I knew that I would not learn the sacred history word for word for anything; there was no point in my even trying to solve the arithmetical problem; as for the Latin third declension, I would probably make a mistake and decline *iteris* instead of *itineris*. . . . A nasty business, but as they say, "one's dream is awful, but God is merciful"—I would run into the kitchen for cool fresh air. . . . There Vasily is preparing to harness the horse and to go fetch my father from work; meanwhile he's reinforcing his vital juices; you can always hear something new from him and enrich your knowledge of unpublishable spoken Russian phrases; or the laundress slips a note into Sergei Ivanych's hands from the master's eldest daughter; or perhaps Sofya Ivanovna has torn herself away from her strict mother and whispers in passing: "Tell him, Apollonochka,[1] that at five o'clock I'll be on the staircase for a minute." But there were times when, after Sergei Ivanych had complained several times about my laziness, my mother wouldn't even let me refresh myself and would make sure that I was sitting next to the window with my book. Then I would sit there, not studying the lesson, but daydreaming; whole novels would be created in my imagination—so alive, although incoherent, that I would feel great tenderness and would weep over imprisoned or persecuted beautiful ladies and heroic knights. I kept my daydreams secret from everyone else, even from Sergei Ivanych, secret because I was ashamed and embarrassed, mainly because I myself was always the hero of these daydreams: I confess that at my age it was inappropriate to have such daydreams. Craftiness, the slave's weapon, developed early in me, and I always pretended that I didn't understand anything indecent. And the truth was, I really didn't completely understand, but I dimly surmised something vaguely, and even though I was only seven or eight years old at the time, this strange feeling always had something to do with women. . . . To make things even more unfortunate, that year, the daughter of my father's neighbor in the country came to visit us for a week. She was given a break from her boarding school; she was around eleven years old, a very pretty little brunette, sharp and lively; that week flew by like a dream, but I recall the memory of it as something warm and sweet, and of the games of hide and seek we played, when Katenka and I would hide in the same place, pressing against each other, and we'd try to conceal our breathing so we wouldn't be heard; about the autumnal twilights together in one armchair, when something ran through my entire body with tingling and sweet sparks. And, it goes without saying, in the novels created in my childish imagination, the captured beauty was none other than Katenka, and I was the chivalrous knight. But I repeat: no one knew about any

1. An affectionate diminutive of the name Apollon.

of this. . . . If I can confess this now—then, to tell the truth—I, just like everyone else, was really indebted for this to Tolstoy,[2] indebted to the new era.

In our time there was no honesty with oneself: a few of us attained sincerity by means of intense effort, but good Lord! It was such a painful process. Even in Tolstoy, whose one foot was anchored in the earlier era, the traces of that painful process are obvious.

But I will return to my own day during that period. Sergei Ivanych would return from the university sooner or later, depending on the number of lectures he attended. He rarely went dressed in his uniform; I never saw any of his comrades, students just like him, wearing uniforms; it seems that neither he nor they ever even owned one. . . . If he came back early, before one o'clock, my lessons would be completed before dinner, that is, before my father returned from his office; if Sergei Ivanych came back late, then it was in the evening, around six o'clock, after tea. In general, there was no established hour for class; the word "class" was never used, and if I hate the classroom order, discipline, and also children's books, it's quite selfless, due to my captious nature. If I had some commission to carry out for Sofya Ivanovna, I would appear with a humbled, but also arrogant face, without knowing my lesson; if not—I would assume a mournful face and would sorrowfully turn in a muddle of numbers instead of the arithmetic problem he'd assigned, would jabber insolently *iter-iteris*, and would incorrigibly confuse Jeroboam with Rehoboam, Ahab with Josaphath.[3] I don't know why Sergei Ivanych constantly repeated that I had great abilities and an excellent heart; I never knew my lessons, and my heart was expressed only in stubborn insolence of lying and in an abundant stream of fake tears. . . . The fact was that Sergei Ivanych, al-

2. A reference to Tolstoy's autobiographical trilogy, *Childhood, Boyhood, and Youth*, which began to appear in 1852.

3. Characters from the Hebrew Bible.

though he was one of the most honest and simple-hearted young men of that era, didn't know how to teach at all; rather, not that he didn't know how to teach, perhaps he did know how, if he would only have rejected the method according to which he himself had studied. . . . But he never dared discard them. He taught me as he himself had been taught: he had been assigned certain passages, and he assigned them to me; Lebedev's Latin grammar had been drummed into his head, and he drummed it into mine. But alas! He never guessed that I had long ago discovered the source of the various Latin themes that were assigned to me from that "hideous book," *De officiis*,[4] although he would walk off into a corner to find an assignment in it, and then, when he went to the university, he would lock the book away in a box under his bed, to which I had obtained a key some time ago, and which later clarified for me many mysteries of nature, when certain color pictures were hidden in it. . . . But just the same, Lebedev's grammar was drummed into me so that there was very little I couldn't understand when Sergei Ivanych conversed in Latin with his friends. I especially understood what I wasn't supposed to. Rozanov's dictionary wasn't fastidious in the least.[5]

At last my father would return from his office around two o'clock, if there were no urgent matters or an inspection. The solemn ceremony called dinner would commence. . . .

Yes! In our house it was indeed a solemn ceremony, for which one had been preparing since morning, carefully ordering dishes and expending all one's intellectual ability making them. This is not yet the place to describe the outrageous lengths the worship of Mammon had attained in our daily life. . . .[6] It had reached its extreme limits in another era, the era of my boyhood and early adolescence. . . .

4. Cicero's primary work about morals (44 BCE).

5. F. F. Rozanov's *Latin Dictionary with Russian Translation* (1797).

6. "Mammon" is a biblical term for riches; here it is used as a false god of wealth.

Dinner would come to an end and, after a short interval, our studies would begin again, lasting more or less not according to the degree of my success, but according to my culpability, so that it always appeared in the form of punishment. It was a strange system, but the fact was that it was administered not according to any system, but simply just so.

I would spend the evening, that is, an ordinary evening, a weekday evening, on the rug in the hall, where, satiated by servants and overwhelmed by my toys, I found myself more interested in the real people around me, in their joys and sorrows . . . in playing cards with them, especially so-called *kings*, and secretly also *noses*, in which I was insulted if my gentry nose was spared when it was the culprit; or we played blind man's bluff, hide and seek, and so forth. But often all of that would bore me: I was oppressed by some strange kind of morbid melancholy. . . .

At nine o'clock people would usually go in to have their supper and this would take more than an hour; all that time I would sit in the dining room, where the reading of various novels by Ann Radcliffe and Madame Cottin would take place.[7]

At ten o'clock I was sent to bed, but the reading continued in the next room, and I never fell asleep before it ended, that is, around one or two o'clock in the morning.

That was a special world, a special life, unlike reality; it was a life of dreams and imagination, a strange life, as powerful in its influence as so-called reality itself.

7. See part 2, chapter I for Ann Radcliffe; Sophie Cottin (1770–1807) was a French writer of romantic intrigues; her novels were very popular in the nineteenth century, and many were translated into Russian.

III

My Teacher's Comrades

Yes! I remember you well, very well, my tutor's small, low, adjacent room, with a window facing a little "gallery," above which was another gallery, the attic staircase leading to the attic ladies, the landlady's daughters—a room with awfully colorless wallpaper, a leather sofa chewed up by innumerable cockroaches, and a portrait of some "mysterious nun" in an old faded gilt frame over that antediluvian sofa. . . . Toward evening Sergei Ivanovich, in the hour "between the wolf and the dog,"[1] before the candles were lit, would lie down on the sofa with me next to him. He would usually put his small, soft hand in my hair, play with it, and recount ancient history to me or fantasize on themes, most of which were quite strange. Since he was so unnaturally impressionable, it wasn't surprising that he listened to my father's reading of novels by Ann Radcliffe or Ducray-Duminil: he himself always wished to become the hero of some mysterious story

1. A French expression, "entre chien et loup," meaning "twilight hours."

and for some reason he would involve me in these wild, incoherent stories.[2]

But I will relate more about him and our strange conversations later.

Toward evening his room became the meeting place almost every day of students, my tutor's comrades. At one time they liked him a great deal, although he didn't stand out by any special talent; they would come to visit him because he rarely ventured out of the house himself. In general, he behaved himself in an exemplary manner for a long time.

As I've already said, he was very young and, the main thing, he was malleable as wax. Besides that, his father and other relatives had placed him in a family house known for the strictness of its morals as well as its warmth and hospitality; they placed him, so to speak, so he would be supervised by a man who in his own circle was considered something of a shining beacon on the basis of his intelligence and education, who even spoke French frequently with counselors of the provincial administration or even with vice-governors themselves, and who would carry out annual so-called inspections of that extremely vile and unattractive place known as the Moscow Magistrate.[3]

My father really had what he'd called "l'ascendant" over his comrades and even more so over the very young tutor. . . . And then my late father loved to use (often abuse) and to demonstrate this influence he had. . . . Intelligent and good by nature, he based his influence not on his intelligence and good heart, but on his bad French and the shreds of an entirely superficial education, received in the university school for noblemen. . . . In addition to that, there was firmly rooted in his nature, as there was in the natures of our entire family, the honor of the gentry;

2. François Guillaume Ducray-Duminil (1761–1819) was a popular French novelist, poet, and songwriter.

3. Introduced in the Russian Empire in 1864 as part of the judicial reforms of Aleksander II. It was based on the British justice of the peace. Grigoryev's father served in this office.

it may have been so firmly rooted that its origin, that class honor, wasn't lost in obscurity like the headwaters of the Nile, but quite simply was derived from the clergy on the male side of the family, and from emancipated serfs on the female side.

And that was a strange business! Well, it would have been enough if my father, who, in spite of his intelligence, was an extremely prosaic man, had been infected by this class honor! But even my older aunt, exalted to the point where she understood many elevated things, read Pushkin with enthusiasm and repeated "Nalivaiko's Confession" with ardor,[4] she too hid the sources of the Nile from herself, while my uncle, whose head was sufficiently sensitive to engage in any sort of freethinking, couldn't stand those sources. I'm convinced that if these pages of mine were to be read now by my elder aunt, who herself might not suspect how much influence she had on my adolescent development with her exaltation that was so strange in its form, but passionate and noble—I'm convinced, I repeat, that my plebian sincerity would produce a very unpleasant impression on her.

I've gone on about this in order to explain the character of my father's "l'ascendant," on my tutor, and on which much depended, practically everything in the tutor's circumstances—on which his friendship also depended. Living in the house, really almost like a member of the family, fed extremely well, though rewarded financially very meagerly, but who had no chance of finding a more lucrative situation—of course, he willy-nilly had to conform to the tastes and customs of the household.

Whoever visited him usually became a friend of the entire family, and therefore would have to adjust "to the household"; and if one didn't fit, it could be said right away that he no longer would be welcome as a guest.

Meanwhile, the university in which my young tutor was enrolled at the end of the 1820s and the beginning of the 1830s

4. An excerpt from an unfinished poem, "Nalivaiko" (1825) by Kondraty Ryleyev (1795–1826), a Russian poet, publisher, and leader of the Decembrist Revolt.

was Moscow University—one replete with tragic repercussions of the recent catastrophe,[5] and terribly receptive to everything unsettled and dizzying that was in the air under the general names of Schellingism in thought and Romanticism in literature, a university of the dying out Polezhayev and others.

I could write a great deal about this turbulent university generation, with which I was well acquainted, but I set myself the task of being the historian only of the tendencies that I myself experienced, to convey their color and smell, as I remember them, and in the order of their impact on me.

It's clear that my tutor Sergei Ivanych wasn't and couldn't be acquainted with Polezhayev and his circle of people who resembled his volcanic personality, both as a result of his mild and weakened nature, and his circumstances, and the nature of "l'ascendant" to which he was subjected.

He didn't find this situation too difficult. "Romanticism" affected his personality only in its comic aspects, that is, more as feelings were involved, and, perhaps, from time to time, as drunkenness was concerned; but "l'ascendant" did not prevent him at all either from standing on the curbstones in the evenings, in front of the windows of small houses of Zamoskvorechye, or from indulging in drunkenness. Adventures were even encouraged by it because they served as a significant source of diversion in his monotonous domestic life. Drunkenness, as is known to everyone, "even to those who haven't studied in a seminary," is after all not considered a sin in ordinary zemstvo life. . . .

It was turbulence, turbulence in its various forms, lack of respect for the existing order. . . . That's what my father was afraid of! Frightened since childhood by the considerable despotism of a strong man that was my grandfather, beaten down morally, though not physically, to the point where he carried no impressions with him from the school for noblemen except for some poetry:

5. The Decembrist Revolt of 1825.

The dancer danced,
While the trunk stood in the corner;[6]

No memories except for the strictness of the inspector, Baron De Villedieu—immediately upon leaving the institution, parting from his friends, many of whom became victims to the catastrophe, and overwhelmed by that same catastrophe to the point of complete incomprehension—and if he wasn't convinced that:

Erudition is a plague, erudition is the cause![7]

On the other hand, he felt completely the profound meaning of the proverb, "A loving calf is suckled by two mothers,"[8] and as a rational, intelligent man he immediately understood the meaning of our social life, where people were very definitely divided into two categories: "big people" and "little people." . . . Well, "a great ship requires deep water," and "little people" have to beware of turbulence all the time.

Naturally, violent people didn't come to visit my tutor—only the meek came; only a few of them in a drunken state, and these had more or less intimate relations with the town police, but even these people were in my father's bad graces and were sent away either by skillful politics, or—alas! in the case of sudden fits of willfulness—with harsher measures, from severe warnings to Sergei Ivanovich, to brutal outbursts, generally characteristic of the eccentric, although of a breed that doesn't bear grudges.

But my father didn't interfere with these humble, "tender" hearts in any way. On the contrary, he himself would come in, joke around with them, tell them endless, interesting tales of life under Catherine II, Paul I, and 1812, and sit there until almost midnight in a cloud of tobacco smoke, which you could

6. Verses said to be written by Lev Tolstoy. The next two lines are as follows: "The dancer didn't notice, / He stumbled and fell."

7. An inexact quotation from Griboyedov's *Woe from Wit.*

8. The Russian proverb continues, "but an obdurate calf gets none."

cut with a knife, in that little room—and he would even invite a few of his favorites, so to speak, into the main rooms of the house—and treat them to "festive," not ordinary, tea, around seven o'clock in the evening. . . .

He did this because these lads were all proper, compliant, and well-behaved. Many of them even shone with pleasing talents—a guitar passed from hand to hand, and their young healthy voices, with the grace of a church choir, and with a kind of melancholy, assumed more for the style, so to speak. They sang either:

> On an inclement autumn evening
> The maiden walked in deserted places . . .[9]

Or, "I part, my angel, from you,"[10] or else, with particular sentiment:

> Don't be amazed, friends,
> Why among you
> At a gay feast,
> I frequently sink
> Into deep thought.[11]

Or the well-known, deeply moving, Ukrainian folk motif to which Raich's song is still sung in every ancient *simandro* (seminary), "The long journey has ended, ended . . ."[12] in every lackey's hall, if such places haven't disappeared yet from the face of the earth. . . . My father, and this was really one of his very good traits, as many of his good qualities will emerge during the course of this truthful narrative, loved large trilling folk songs, but would listen with pleasure to these romances that

9. The first lines of a popular romance (1827) by Pushkin.

10. The first lines of an eighteenth-century folk romance.

11. The refrain of a song "To My Friends" (1827) by Semyon Raich (1792–1855), a Russian poet and translator.

12. The beginning of a romance by Alexander Durop (1818).

were very popular at the time. In her good moments, my mother also passionately loved music and singing.

All of this was splendid; the young people's good morality, meekness, their songs, and their innocent, amorous adventures, appropriate at their age, to which my father, who had already started living only in his reminiscences, listened with great curiosity, occasionally repeating that routine saying: "That's the sort we are!" and which I, hiding away in some dark corner, was secretly listening to with strange anxiety. . . . All this was splendid, I repeat. . . . And my father, protecting Sergei Ivanych from violent people, and satisfying his own taste for peaceful manners, had in mind, undoubtedly, also to instill in me good morals, obedience to elders, the deference essential in life, and other virtues.

But there is something in the infinite, eternally ironic, and omnipotent force called life, something that constantly, insidiously destroys all serene Arcadias; there are irresistibly enticing, head-spinning whirlwinds, which raising waves on the broad seas, do so at the same time on rivers, rivulets, even little streams and brooks, and don't even leave the bog slime alone—whirlwinds of thought that disturb even the most somnolent tranquility, whirlwinds of poetry that carry away everything before them like a waterfall. . . . Whirlwinds of worldwide historical movements that finally leave behind them terrible monuments of destruction or majestic traces of glory.

Yet, in my tutor Sergei Ivanych's entire circle of comrades, there were, strictly speaking, only two individuals who took life and its demands seriously. One of them was a deeply honest, profoundly humble person,[13] to whom I was subsequently indebted for all the factual knowledge—who went on to bear the cross for serving science with the persistence of love and simple faith. The other one, as best I can recall, took the demands of life seriously, in that he naively, sincerely, and wholeheartedly

13. Most likely Ivan Belyayev (1810–1873), a future professor of the history of Russian law at Moscow University.

burned through it to the point of ferocity and disorder, to the point of passion and cynicism. . . . All the others were obviously fated to turn sour, slowly become drunkards, or gradually sink in the muck of various good behaviors.

But how did life's whirlwind grab hold of that circle of mediocrities as well; how did the currents of the era not only touch them, but often even carry them away, only mentally, of course? Surely the reason was that if the conversation grew lively, it didn't concern advantageous positions and future careers. . . . They spoke, and they did so with passion, about the self-taught Polevoy and his journal the *Telegraph* with its romantic aspirations.[14] Every new line written by Pushkin was greedily captured in innumerable almanacs of that naive era; the name "Lord Byron" was uttered with some sort of feverishness. . . . The wild and impetuous poems of Polezhayev were transmitted from mouth to mouth. . . . When that name was uttered—and very rarely, of course—a few others, even more untouchable names,[15] some sort of horror overtook the circle of young men, and at the same time, there was also something awfully seductive, invincibly attractive in this horror, and, if on festive occasions, such as name days, birthdays, and other events that permitted "wine and oil," the company reached a somewhat artificially heightened mood . . . then the undefined feeling of superstitious and, at the same time, fascinating fear was replaced by some kind of desperate, naive sympathy—both for those speeches, whose . . .

> . . . meaning
> Is obscure or insignificant,
> But that cannot be listened to
>
> Without strong emotion,[16]

14. Nikolai Polevoy (1796–1846) was a Russian journalist, critic, and historian.
15. A reference to the Decembrist writers, Ryleyev and Bestuzhev-Marlinksy.
16. A quotation from the poem, "There Are Speeches" (1840) by Mikhail Lermontov (1814–1841).

and in those people, who either "burned life" selflessly, or who boldly staked it on a playing card. . . . Then some sort of strange speeches were heard, as if not even their own words, from the mouths of these moral young men. . . .

How, even in their sober moments, they told each other stories about their terrible comrades, who devoted their heads and hearts to the moral intoxication of Schellingism or else all their lives to their raging passions! After all, all these well-behaved young men knew very well that to surrender themselves completely to that sort of thinking couldn't lead to anything positive. Some of them even attempted to treat philosophical or life-frenzy humorously—saying that "they were losing their marbles"—nevertheless, they surrendered anxiously to the fascination.

It wasn't the *European Herald*, but the *Telegraph* with its vague, but vital aspirations that fervently divided young people. . . . They listened attentively not to professors of the old school, but were carried away fanatically, carried away to the point of *autos ephē*, by the breadth of Nadezhdin's literary views (then expressed only in his lectures), by Pavlov's fantastic, yet highly promising world order, in his physics; and so almost all these young people, with the exception of one (a future toiler in history), were enrolled in medical school, and were carried away by the song of its siren, Dyadkovsky.[17] That name resounded daily in my ears; it was surrounded by the most slavish respect, and it was also the name of the struggle between the new vital science and the old routine. As a nonspecialist, of course I can't judge very well Dyadkovsky's worth, but I know only that discussions

17. "Autos ephē" (Gk.) translates to "he said so himself"; it is a proverbial phrase used to characterize statements made without argumentation based on reason or evidence. Mikhail Pavlov (1792–1840) was a Russian professor at Moscow University, largely responsible for spreading the philosophical ideas of the *Naturphilosophie* of Schelling. "Future toiler in history" refers to Belyayev. Iyustin Dyadkovsky (1784–1841) was an inspirational teacher and professor of medicine at Moscow University.

with him lasted well beyond the normal class period, and that all these young people without exception listened spellbound to his "powerful words," just as later, we of the next generation, also greedily directed our eyes and ears to the lectern, long after the bell rang, where, with somewhat exaggerated effects, and perhaps even a little charlatanism, the words of the great teacher from Berlin, reverberated to us.

How, I repeat, these people whom the muck of philistinism awaited in the future, or whose fate would make them lifelong habitual drinkers, how they were completely carried away by the tendencies of philosophy and poetry, the new, bold aspirations of science, who were proudly building a whole world solely by means of transcendental thinking derived from a simple all-embracing principle.

Temptation, terrible temptation was wafting in the air, resounding with Pushkin's passionately sweet verse. Temptation was bursting into our life in the form of the whirlwinds of Young France's literature. . . . The generation that had grown up wasn't seeking a point of serenity or support, but was only tempted by turbulent sensations. The generation that was still growing up, having inhaled the air poisoned by these sensations, greedily longed for life, passions, battles, and suffering.

Since my reminiscences are connected only by chronological order and since this section begins directly with a sketch of the literary period of the 1830s, I don't consider it necessary to refer to the opening chapters in which I outlined my impressions of my infancy. [Author's note.]

IV

Something Extremely Scandalous about Tendencies in General

If one were to think back some thirty odd years, even a man who'd lived through these same thirty years will suddenly feel somewhat strange, as if he'd set foot in a neighborhood where he hadn't been for many years, and where everything was frozen in the same form in which it had been left by him—so while looking closely at objects, he gradually reproduces his previous impressions of these objects with greater and greater clarity, gradually recalls their taste, color, and smell, while at the same time he very clearly feels that this long-since previous life arises before him as some sort of fantastically real mirage.

But the attitude to that outdated form of human life must seem even stranger to someone of another, later generation when he sees before him only its dead, printed monuments, and at that, of course, not all of them . . . yes, perhaps not even those in which that outdated era was depicted unconditionally and spontaneously, and made its appearance before the most esteemed public not in a frockcoat and white gloves, but in ordinary clothing, as if it had just risen from bed, leading with its left or right foot.

No longer ago than yesterday evening, oh my dear Horatio with a pigtail,[1] while talking with you after the concert where we heard the second symphony of the old master,[2] who while composing it had not yet become deaf to contemporary and earlier dining room chamber music, but who'd already sown handfuls of his own profound thoughts and his pantheistic reflections on life in it, attempting to clarify the meaning of these obvious "encounters" of something deeply serious and grave that sound in the unexpected piercing notes of the violins and cellos in the *allegro patetico*,[3] searching for, or rather, seizing upon the meaning of the slower measures in the finale, measures that were clearly marked with some gloomy and imposing idea, measures that recur, though no longer as precisely, in the subsequent development of the musical fabric; no longer ago than yesterday, I say, we spoke about those tendencies that are so amusing to our contemporary thinkers.

There is not the slightest doubt that they found them amusing, just as there can't be any doubt that the mental mastication, which they feed to their adepts, is incomparably more accessible than our transcendental ravings, nevertheless (I'm entirely in agreement with the principles expressed in your last letter) that if transcendental ideas arise in the brains of "degenerate apes," which is what ignoramuses who haven't read Moleschott and other wise men usually call people,[4] one can't help sending them to those "particular individuals," with whom Mephistopheles's key acquainted Goethe's Faust, and if that proves to be impossible, then we have the absolute right to live out our lives as transcendentalists. And even then, to tell the truth, if you and I, ashamed to some extent

1. "Pigtail" (*kositsa*) was the pseudonym of Nikolai Strakhov in Dostoevsky's journals. Strakhov (1828–1896), was a Russian philosopher, publicist, journalist, and literary critic, as well as a good friend of Grigoryev's.
2. Ludwig van Beethoven.
3. A reference to the fourth movement of Beethoven's Symphony No. 2: *allegro molto*.
4. Strakhov's letter to the editor published in the journal *Epoch* (1864). Jacob Moleschott (1822–1893) was a Dutch physiologist and writer known for his philosophical views in regard to scientific materialism.

of our groundlessness before the great contemporary thinkers, were to repeat to each other Famusov's words to Chatsky:

> Get rid of these jumbled notions,

then we would probably burst out laughing immediately like some Roman augurs. Therefore, transcendentalism is sort of a notch made by Lyubim Tortsov,[5]

> if you land on that notch, you won't easily jump off.

Indeed, you won't jump off at all. I have a friend, whom you also know, a man of the generation that came between the transcendentalists and the nihilists, so to speak, who is completely satisfied with Beneke's fragmentary psychological contrivances, which have so little interest for the two of us.[6] Once, in an earnest conversation, he happened to recount a particular psychological experiment, extremely curious and even instructive. He undertook to read Schelling's *System of Transcendental Idealism* with the firm intention of studying it thoroughly in order to acquire a conclusive view of that philosophy,[7] which, though outdated, is still important in the history of philosophical thought. Well, as you know, outdated doctrine immediately shocks one with its paradoxical results, with the necessity either to derive the entire creation of the world out of the laws of the conscious "I," or else the conscious "I" from the laws of the creation of the world. Of course, in essence, it doesn't matter, and that's exactly

5. A reference to Alexander Ostrovsky's comedy *Poverty Is No Vice* (1853).
6. The friend referred to, Yevgeny Edelson (1824–1868), was a Russian literary critic and translator and a supporter of Beneke's who was an opponent of rationalism and Hegelianism. Friedrich Beneke (1798–1854) was a German psychologist and post-Kantian philosopher, who maintained that the basis of all philosophy is to be found in empirical psychology.
7. Published in 1800 in which Schelling described transcendental philosophy and nature philosophy as complementary to one another. His work exerted a great influence on the development ofRomanticism.

why there appears a philosophy of identity; but the paradox in the first instance strikes one like that wall, which the hero of our friend Fyodor Dostoevsky confronts.[8] My friend studied ardently and read carefully, with the same ardor and care with which he conquered Beneke's *Psychological Sketches* and his other acts of mental masturbation. He had already also begun digesting as the process in which from our immediate, so to speak, objective "I," there stands out another "I" in which the subject of cognition of "I," a conscious "I" is detached from another "I" that is aware of external subjects—and to a certain extent judges that same "I" that is conscious of external subjects, in which, finally. . . . But here my extremely careful friend, who is reasonable and not at all contemptuous of life's comforts, caught himself in time, guessed that he had come into contact with a sphere where things begin to turn upside down, and that, from that judging "I," which produces both judgment and punishment, by some sort of acknowledged rules, made a mark, perhaps, after making many such marks, such an "I," that does not want to have anything to do with any laws except identity of the world, a transcendental "I," extremely dangerous and immoral.

And my prudent friend closed the evil book and in so doing he saved for his fatherland a useful member as a good paterfamilias, who only from time to time, in view of life's necessary variety, allows himself several sprees; and finally he became a figure in the literary field, "like a clerk who's turned gray in his office,"[9] who can

> Serenely gaze upon the innocent and the guilty,[10]

without getting carried away, and without falling into error in his judgments—which you and I, oh, my dear Horatio, will never be!

8. In *Notes from Underground* (1863), chapter 3 of part 1.

9. An inexact quotation from Pushkin's verse tragedy *Boris Godunov* (1825).

10. From the same source: Gregory's description of the monk Pimen.

And truly, what sort of passion has developed in you and me, what sort of irregular vein throbs in us, people of a "transcendental" disposition, that we find it so terribly boring to read Beneke, who is completely clear and proceeds according to the methodology of natural science, while it's not at all boring to split one's head reading *The Phenomenology of the Spirit.*[11] But it's not that it's boring to read Beneke: it's just that it requires enormous effort; if you find it boring, you, who wrote a master's thesis on certain *infusoria* bones,[12] unknown to anyone except under a microscope, or on some subject just as unlikely—after all, I'm an arrogant humanist and I myself know that I'm revealing my terrible ignorance; but if you do not, I repeat, find it so, then it cost me incredible efforts to catch Beneke's ideas by the tail,[13] for example—and even here it seems that my attempt to catch them is completely useless, and that in the opinion of my Benekian, I'm studying not what I should be, and that I should seek out the general tail, from which emerge all the little tails as if from the center, like little snakes, because, if you will, why is that central tail necessary? All-embracing principles turned out to be completely insubstantial.

But let me be permitted to jump across time and space in this entirely scandalous and indecently eccentric chapter—to gallop over the former and to forget completely about the existence of the latter. . . .

At this point I recall the time when, after heeding the advice of my reasonable friend, I undertook the study of psychological sketches with zeal worthy of a better fate. I didn't decide to do so because my friend was particularly influential on me in our conversations. In fact, my friend was very eloquent in his explanation of the parallelism between psychological and phys-

11. One of Hegel's major treatises (1807).

12. *Infusoria* are minute freshwater life forms. It's a putdown of Strakhov's dissertation.

13. Friedrich Eduard Beneke (1798–1854) was a German psychologist and post-Kantian philosopher.

ical phenomena, about foundations and spiritual formations; my friend carried on these conversations even with beautiful, clever ladies—and of course, not without success, although, unfortunately, this success was not at all scientific, because the beautiful, clever ladies while listening to him, were looking more at his eyes, which at that time were very clear and blue, and from his logical eloquence, they drew a completely illogical premise about other, so to speak, vile characteristics of his nature, but ladies are all like that in general; and it is doubtful that even cutting off their braids, or arguments about female labor will save them from such thinking. . . . I was fascinated not by my friend's eloquence, and not even by him, but by the "tendency," of which he was one of the enthusiastic representatives at the time.

This took place at the beginning of the 1850s, at the time of my second and genuine youth, at the time when there arose in my soul a new or, better to say, renewed faith in the ground, soil, and people, at a time when everything was re-created in my mind and heart, everything that reflection and science had only seemed to wipe out in them, at a time of fresh hopes, like the green cover of our dear journal, *The Muscovite* of 1851. . . . My soul was revived . . . and I believed . . . and with all haste, I rushed to meet those great discoveries that shone forth at the beginning of Ostrovsky's career, to those fresh springs that appeared in Pisemsky's *Idler* and other works,[14] and in the clearly talented a secret place, arose a world of legends, rejected only logically by reflection, and the walls of the old Kremlin, and the artless highly artistic pages of the ancient chronicles; they spoke to me again, as in the years of my childhood, of the organic world of folk poetry. I was beginning to be reborn in loneliness—I, who had for several years been leading someone else's life, definitely not experiencing my own, but someone else's passions, and I began to search for my own self in the depths of my soul.

14. Aleksey Pisemsky (1821–1881) was a Russian novelist and dramatist, regarded as an equal of Ivan Turgenev and Fyodor Dostoevsky in the late 1850s.

The spirit of this new time attracted me with irresistible force. There's something almost ridiculously naive and, at the same time, something almost touching in that fanatical belief with which I was trying to rush ahead, as we all were, rushing ahead anyway, even though we thought we were turning back. . . . Such a faith won't ever be experienced again, and although it's foolish to regret that, it's still a pity that it can't be experienced! That was all as fine as a sunrise, as sparkling pollen on flower petals.

Fanatical, such as some Seids in the Muslim faith, I was ready to confess my transcendental process like some sort of sin, and while it caused my soul some pain, I was capable of denying it, as denying "Satan and all his deeds." But, alas! Two things turned out to be very clear: the first was that once one has reached that point where, according to my friend's conception, nature turns upside down—one has to repeat with the poet:

> *Per me si va nell' eterno dolore. . . .*
> *Lasciate ogni speranza, voi ch'entrete!*[15]

And the second thing is that Beneke's psychological masturbations were as inappropriate to the new tendency of life, as a "saddle would be on a cow. . . ." Beneke ended up in the "circle" completely by chance, and if the Petersburg critics began to reproach the representatives of the circle for their "fundamentals," they certainly didn't mean the kind that exist in the *Psychological Sketches* and other works of the learned psychologist (my tongue refuses to call him a philosopher).

But with what "triumphant elegance," so to speak, my friend approached me, carrying a copy of Beneke's *Sketches* for me. In the first place, as I now remember clearly, he interrogated me:

15. From Dante's *Inferno*, canto 3, line 2, "Through me is the way to eternal sorrow"; and line 9, "Abandon all hope, ye who enter here."

Did I engage in psychological experiences galvanically,[16] to burrow into my own soul and those of other featherless bipeds, especially those of the feminine gender? This also occurred frequently, but it was not the sort of psychological work and psychological observations that my friend had in mind. He very rightly called a life that was experienced galvanically "phony," and often, as a man, fortunately, who was little involved in it, he related to it humorously; as for my observations of the better half of the biped species, as well as in his virtue not abiding my sophistical conversations with women that were directed toward practical ends, he referred to them as a "hussar relationship," only "lifted into the pearl of consciousness and delicacy of feelings. . . ."[17] Therefore, for a long time I didn't understand what sort of psychological studies he expected from me. In any case, I set about studying Beneke with hardened stubbornness and even submitted myself blindly to his guidance. He didn't place *Lehrbücher*,[18] that is, his system, in my hands, justifiably suspecting that I wanted to grasp the principle tail, and in part fearing that in the textbooks, I would soon grasp the little tails therefore only superficially.

Therefore, although my friend turned back from a particular point in transcendentalism, yet as an exceptionally intelligent man he understood completely the lecherously profound and the simultaneously profoundly lecherous thought of the great teacher in *The Phenomenology of the Spirit*, that only the process itself is important in thinking, and that the result is nothing but a lifeless corpse, abandoned by the living soul—by tendency.

So at that time I used to spend long winter evenings reading the *Psychological Sketches* of the German Herr Professor and torment my poor brain over it not in order to understand what I

16. Grigoryev means "artificially aroused." Luigi Galvani (1737–1798) was an Italian physician, physicist, biologist, and philosopher, who studied animal electricity.

17. A quotation from Nikolai Gogol's novel, *Dead Souls*.

18. Textbooks (Ger.).

was reading, because all that material, taken irrespectively, was very simple, but in order to concentrate fully on my reading. Meanwhile, behind the wall, suddenly, as if in derision . . .

> Two guitars, striking up,
> Began to moan plaintively.[19]

The Hungarian dance's rebellious shiver runs across the strings, or the rustle of a young girl's light steps sounds above the ceiling, and the soul hungrily begins to seek life, life, and still more life. . . . Thus I sat for several evenings, and then returned the book to my friend with the most naive realization that I couldn't possibly force myself to take an interest in it. He sees that there's nothing to be done with the likes of me, a lost soul. He purchased and gave me a *Lehrbuch.* I read it very quickly; I absorbed all that mechanical business, so to speak, and I began appropriately to argue clearly enough, though superficially, about that new system. . . . "That's enough for me!" I thought, because its adherents are forbidden to catch its absolute tail. And the devil with it, if I couldn't catch that tail at all.

Why did this happen during the time of my early youth and when all my physical forces and aspirations were still totally fresh, on some clear, teasing, inviting spring morning to the peal of Moscow's church bells at Easter? You sit there engrossed in reading this or that deranged attempt to seek the absolute tail. . . . You sit there, and your head would burn and your heart would beat—not from the summons of spring and life bursting through the open window with vanilla-scented, narcotic air . . . but from those enormous worlds, connected by the unity built by organic thought; or you rummage painfully in rising doubts, capable of destroying the entire structure of spiritual and moral beliefs . . . and you would fall physically ill, grow thin, and turn

19. A quotation from "The Hungarian Gypsy Dance." This very popular romance was composed by Ivan Vasiliev (1810–1870) to the words of Grigoryev's poem.

sallow from this process. . . . Oh! these torments and aches of the soul—how disgustingly sweet they were! Oh! these sleepless nights, when one would fall to one's knees with a sob and pray fervently, and immediately the capacity for prayer would be undermined by analysis—nights of mental frenzy right up to the dawn and the tolling of matins—oh, they raised the spiritual disposition so very high!

And then I recall how at the end of 1856, when I was lying sick in bed—having already survived my second youth, broken morally and physically—one of the good old Mohicans, the famous Don Basilio Pedro, sent me for consolation the introductory volume, just published, of Schelling's *Philosophy of Mythology*.[20] The noble Don was afraid to visit me because I had a late case of smallpox, but he sent the book with a note; in it, in passing, he mentioned that he had already sniffed the book, and it smelled rather fragrant. . . . I affixed my sickly, weak eyes onto the mysteriously sweet-smelling book—and once again the powerful tendency of thought drew me after itself—and my late father, who was tending to me like a nurse, had to take that "wicked blight" away from me by force.

In the garden of an Italian villa located near the *Tomba tusca*,[21] I sat for hours at a time with that "wicked blight" and its succeeding volumes; once again my head burned and my heart was pounding, as in my student days—and neither the fragrance of roses and lemons, nor the fear of tarantulas, about whose presence at Etruscan graves I'd been warned by the staid Englishman Belle, my student Prince Trubetskoy's tutor—nothing could distract me.

The transcendental tendency, *sub alia forma*,[22] seized me again and enthralled me.

---

20. Don Basilio Pedro, a lighthearted nickname for Vasily Botkin, who had published his *Letters about Spain* in 1857. Schelling's *Philosophy of Mythology* was published in 1856.

21. "Etruscan gravesite" (It.).

22. "Among other things" (Lat.).

V

Literary Tendencies at the Beginning of the 1830s

Of course, I didn't write the previous chapter "simply for the sake of scandal," although according to my own admission, it turned out to be quite scandalous.

I wanted somehow to depict visually, in general aspects, "for the consolation of my contemporaries and the edification of posterity," the power and influence of transcendentalism on the people of my generation, in order to clarify somewhat its power and influence on the generation preceding ours.

At the same time I also wanted to expound as truthfully as possible my beliefs in the relationship to what I have grown used to calling the "tendencies of life," to expound on it directly and boldly, perhaps for the amusement and mockery of our positivists and nihilists. . . .

Yes! Historically speaking it isn't we, who live "as individuals," but what lives are "tendencies," of which we, individuals, are more or less significant representatives. . . . From this stems the extremely obvious parallelism of events in various spheres of earthly life—the strange, mysterious coincidence of the simultaneous creation of Don Quixote and Hamlet, revolutionary tendencies and Beethoven's compositions, etc., etc. . . . From this stems the solidarity of certain ideas, their universal sequential connection, and who knows what else stems from it, friend Horatio,

> Than are dreamt of in your philosophy,[1]

and that it rejects merely because it didn't catch a sufficient number of little tails and thus, didn't reach the tail common to all.

The power lies in the fact that transcendentalism was a *force*, a tendency, that was carrying off with it all that could have been thought in those days. All that could only have been felt was carried away by another tendency, which, as a result of the lack of another word, must be called Romanticism. In essence, one and the other—transcendentalism and romanticism, were two sides of one and the same idea. Incidentally, I've argued and written so much on the subject that if I were to start doing so again, it would only inevitably fall into the category of repetition.

Therefore, in order to clarify for my readers the essence of the romantic tendency, I choose the path of narration, rather than argumentation.

Let's transport ourselves to the end of the 1820s and the beginning of the 1830s. Onstage in front of us, in the first place, appears the great and almost completely clear physiognomy of the first person, who completely expressed our essence: Pushkin. He'd matured well before "Poltava"—in his briefcase there already lies what he'd called (according to legend), a "hundred thousand and immortality," that is, '"a comedy about Boris Godunov and Grishka Otrepyev," but his character is still illuminated by a purely romantic halo, and young people still see the Byron in him.[2] He has yet to smile with the good-natured, yet simultaneously sar-

1. An inaccurate quotation from *Hamlet*, act 1, scene 5.
2. "Poltava" (1828–1829), a long narrative poem, centers on a historical figure, the Ukrainian hetman Mazepa in the 1709 Battle of Poltava between Sweden and Russia.

castic, smile of Ivan Petrovich Belkin, "has not yet written with Karamzin's solemnity," and along with the unusually fine musical beat of reality, about the historical fate of the inhabitants of the village of Goryukhino, he has not yet looked sympathetically into the life of some stationmaster.[3] He's the idol of the younger generation, but in fact, that generation doesn't see him exactly as he is, and doesn't expect from him what he intends to give. If the younger generation had possessed the gift of farsightedness, it would have recoiled in horror from its idol. It would forgive him the comical story about Count Nulin,[4] it's even ready to see Romanticism in that first simple depiction of our reality, but it won't forgive him for *The Tales of Belkin*. . . .

The younger generation of that time has its own leader and its own dynamic organ, quick on the uptake for anything that is in the air, talented to the point of self-taught genius, easily assimilating, clearly and passionately communicating all of life's tendencies, he himself gets carried away and he carries others away in his wake . . . the "little merchant Polevoy," as he was called on the one hand by impotent old men, and on the other, by literary aristocrats, both foaming at the mouth.

Because both of these generations do indeed exist. They are still alive and will thrive and even publish their own journals: one brought up on pretentious odes—old men in buskins, and the younger generation, steeped through and through in Karamzin's "Poor Liza."[5] The old men wearing "flesh-colored stockings," who, after "Poor Lisa," digested perhaps only Zhukovsky's "Lyudmila," and, like the Chairman in Gogol's *Dead Souls*, read it with eyes half closed and with special emphasis

3. *Tales of Belkin* (1831) is a series of five short stories with a fictional editorial introduction by Pushkin himself. "History of the Village of Goryukhino" (1830) is an unfinished short story.

4. "Count Nulin" (written in1825) is a witty parody of Shakespeare's "The Rape of Lucrece," shows Pushkin at his most lighthearted.

5. Nikolai Karamzin's sentimental tale (1794) about a young peasant girl betrayed by her gentry seducer.

on the word "Hark!"[6] They consider not only the little merchant Polevoy, but even Professor Merzlyakov, at least the older generation does, a heretic for his critical comments about Sumarokov, Kheraskov, and Ozerov. . . .[7] For them, moreover, particularly the first group, there is no other literature besides those "contrived works"; among them, that is, among the miserable buskins and flesh-colored stockings, a mortal struggle is being waged for Karamzin, a subject of horror for the pupils and followers of the author of *On the Old and New Style*, an idol for flesh-colored stockings, reaching the point of the most repulsive idolatry in the person of Ivanchin-Pisarev.[8]

There are also literary aristocrats, grouping themselves around Zhukovsky and Pushkin. They're educated like Europeans, lazy like young Russian noblemen, punctiliously neat in their literary tastes like some English Miss, which, by the way, doesn't prevent them from writing verse whose contents are largely provocative, or from knowing V. L. Pushkin's *Dangerous Neighbor* by heart. . . .[9] Finally, there's still a circle of Polevoy's enemies, formed by young scholars like Pogodin and Shevyryov, of aristocrats, known for the seriousness of their start in life, like Khomyakov, at that time still only a poet, and also I. V. Kireyevsky.[10] This small group of people, advancing onto the

---

6. Vasily Zhukovsky (1783–1852) was the foremost Russian poet in the early nineteenth century, best known for his ballads, of which Lyudmila was the most famous. For the description of the Chairman, see Gogol's *Dead Souls*, chapter 8.

7. Alexander Sumarokov, Mikhail Kheraskov, and Vladislov Ozerov were generally well-regarded classical writers at the end of the eighteenth century.

8. The book referred to is by Admiral Alexander Shishkov (1754–1841), a Russian writer and statesman, whose intense old-fashioned nationalistic and religious sentiments were opposed to Karamzin's new style. Nikolai Ivanchin-Pisarev (1790–1849) was a Russian writer and devoted follower of Karamzin.

9. V. L. Pushkin (1766–1830) was Alexander Pushkin's uncle and the author of a humorous masterpiece, *A Dangerous Neighbor* (1811), set in a bawdyhouse.

10. Mikhail Pogodin (1800–1875) was a historian and journalist; Stepan Shevyryov (1806–1864) was a literary historian, critic, and minor poet; Ivan Kireyevsky (1805–1856) was a literary critic and one of the principal architects of

field of action by Kireyevsky's brilliant article in the almanac *Dawn* and concentrating in the *Moscow Herald*, gravitating for the most part toward Pushkin, and partly toward Zhukovsky, is connected with the circle of literary aristocrats, but finding itself in the most indefinite relationship to the old men in buskins and those in flesh-colored stockings: respect for tradition ties that group to them; the cult of Pushkin divides them from it. However, in one respect it is in complete agreement with them—in hostility toward Polevoy. The literary aristocrats and Pushkin himself keep away from this battle. Even Pushkin's poems and those of his friends appear at times in the plebian *Telegraph*, but the old men and the isolated circle are raging.

From our present point of view, if would be impossible to imagine anything more indecent than that article, with which the editor of the *Moscow Herald* burst out against *The History of the Russian People*,[11] if the articles against it in the *European Herald* hadn't been even more indecent.

I repeat, from our present point of view, all of these enmities and literary ragings are incomprehensible. It will be even less understandable when one comes to know the personalities of those involved. . . . The author of *The History of the Russian People* was Polevoy; the editor of the *Moscow Herald* was Pogodin.

The actors are not presented at all in their normal order some thirty years ago. What was the reason they were so hostile to each other that they foamed at the mouth? The merchant Polevoy, susceptible to all the tendencies of contemporary life, was not a Westernizer at all, but a full-fledged Russian man, and least of all, a negator of the idea of national character. On the other hand, Pogodin was always a democrat to his fingertips—and what was there for him to share with that other democrat, Polevoy?

Slavophilism; Aleksey Khomyakov was a Russian theologian, philosopher, poet, and amateur artist. He cofounded the Slavophile movement along with Kireyevsky.

11. Written by Polevoy in 1829 to refute Karamzin's *History of the Russian State* (1818).

Yes, that's the way it seems to us now that there was nothing to be shared. In the course of thirty years the two sides were mixed up and kept changing places; and there were enough changes in order to be able to establish their mutual relations correctly, at least to some extent.

Now it's easy for us to pass judgment on one actor or another, just as it's easy to laugh at the dedication of *The History of the Russian People* to Niebuhr,[12] who, of course, couldn't read it, and to laugh, on the other hand, at the cult that was created for Karamzin by his followers, people who really, sincerely, and profoundly experienced the "spirit" of the Karamzinian era and carried the trace of that tendency in them for many decades: in other words, that's how strong it was. . . .

After all, even Polevoy, in spite of his subsequent, unfortunate, dramatic activity, to which he was compelled by circumstances, and Pogodin, in spite of his passionate and incomprehensible enthusiasm for nature's means of expression—were both fighters for an honorable, noble cause, fighters, of whom much will be forgiven because "they loved much. . . ." Neither one nor the other was at fault that, seized by various "tendencies," they grew antagonistic toward each other, just as later the Slavophiles and Belinksy were not to blame for the same reasons.

But thirty years ago the facts were such that the merchant was the representative of, so to speak, contemporary throbbing interests of life, or, if you like, the mirage of life at that time; his enemies seemed to the large part of the younger generation to be backward people. What difference does it make if the advanced people soon "went crazy," to such a degree that they couldn't understand the sublime sphere of Pushkin's development, or that the backward people kept going forward steadily and finally degenerated into Slavophilism, which was clearly triumphant in

12. Barthold Niebuhr (1776–1831) was a Danish-German statesman who became Germany's leading historian of ancient Rome and was a founding father of modern historiography.

many respects? After thirty years, the facts, I repeat, appear as I have shown them, and we have to accept them as the starting point, if we wish to understand that former period properly.

Yes, indeed! It's not for naught, for instance, that I mentioned such monuments of certain literary epochs, in which they, that is, the epochs themselves, appear undressed before the observer, as if they'd just gotten out of bed.

In the *Telegraph* of 1830, namely, in volume 35 (I checked it in the public library, but forgot to note the page number), if you look in the section of "Miscellany," you will find articles about the theater signed with the two letters V. U., and you will unintentionally stumble across a comparatively long article about Molière's comedy, *The Miser*, in Russian translation and on the Russian production. . . . If you don't read between the lines, you won't understand a thing in this daring, intelligent article, which was written with frightful fervor. The article tears to shreds, mercilessly at that—in a way comparable to the cynicism of the "civic-minded" publications of the day—some nobleman, a member of all possible private clubs, an inevitable partner in games of whist and Boston, acquainted with the circle of literary and literary-official nobility, but who, meanwhile, out of dilettantism and idleness, deems himself worthy of engaging with the theater and literature, and is in general even full of pretensions about it, claiming considerable significance for himself and his occupations. Then there follows criticism of the translation of Molière's comedy, which is abusive to the point of captiousness and captious to the point of abuse. Even for a person not familiar with the mysteries of literature of that time, two facts are obvious: (1) that the nobleman torn to shreds and the translator of *The Miser* are one and the same; and (2) that the biliously furious and bloody article is a result of long, stubborn, tone-deaf, open warfare between the two parties.

In order to show you at once what the point is, and the essence of the article, I will name only the author of the angry article and the translator of the comedy, and send you off to check it in one single book, which is quite easy to locate.

The translator of Moliere's *L'Avare* is Sergei Aksakov. The columnist in the *Telegraph* is Vasily Ushakov. The book to which I am referring is Aksakov's *Collection of Various Theatrical and Literary Reminiscences.*

You probably know both Sergei Aksakov and his books already,[13] if you haven't limited your reading to five well-known clever little books, but even in that case, you would have at least heard something about them. But you probably don't know Vasily Ushakov, who wrote only one remarkable thing, and only "remarkable" at that time; it was the little tale, "Kirghiz-Kaisak."[14] You, you "five-booker," don't know this thing at all, and you'll probably pride yourself on your ignorance; if you're neither fish nor fowl, that is, neither us, people of a bygone era, nor people of the latest five books, you'll recall that name vaguely together with a dirty, grayish cover of some textbook of Russian literature of days gone by—well, say it's the nice book by Mr. Georgievsky, if you like, which is equally enthusiastic about Pushkin's *Boris Godunov* and Mr. Kukolnik's *Tasso*—an extremely instructive textbook as proof of the victory achieved by romantic ideas of the 1830s; it's a textbook that astonishingly combined the most old-fashioned principles of "semandrics" with Polevoy's critical views—and, even now, puts onto his pages Senkovsky-Brambeus's unedited whistle.[15]

Therefore I am first of all obliged to inform you that Vasily Ushakov, in addition to writing "Kirghiz-Kaisak," which created a considerable stir in literary circles in its own time, also wrote

13. Aksakov's principle work is titled *My Literary and Moral Reminiscences* (1858).

14. Ushakov's "Kirghiz-Kaisak." was published in 1830.

15. *Handbook for the Study of Russian Literature* (1842) by Pyotr Georgievsky. Nestor Kukolnik (1809–1868) was a Russian playwright and prose writer of Carpatho-Rusyn origin. His fantasy drama, *Torquato Tasso*, resulted in his being regarded as a legendary playwright in the capital. "Senkovsky-Brambeus's unedited whistle" is an ironic reference to the foundations of the seminarian's aesthetics. Osip Ivanovich Senkovsky (1800–1858), was a Polish-Russian orientalist, journalist, and entertainer; under the pen name Baron Brambeus, he published a series of fantastic voyages.

a regular column in the *Telegraph*, which created an even bigger stir than his tale; he was an extremely broadly educated man with a very sharp wit. . . .

And now, I really don't know how best to show you the very strange position of the two sides on the chessboard. It would be best of all if I present their final, latter positions *ex abrupto.*[16]

Vasily Ushakov subsequently wrote *The Tomcat Burmosek*, a work far less talented than the inventions of Fedot Kuzmichev, Sigov, and other merchants at Moscow's rag market. In addition, in the *Library for Reading*, then already in its decline, when Nadezhdin in the *Telescope* and Shevyrev in the *Observer* destroyed the temporary idol of the youth of Petersburg, Brambeus, he wrote an absolutely despicable work with the title *Visyasha*,[17] something on the order of an untalented and completely nonsensical denunciation of the immorality of aesthetic teachings, whose fiery sermon the great fighter, Vissarion Belinsky, had just begun in the pages of the *Word*, under the title *Literary Reveries.*

Sergei Aksakov was ending his career—perhaps you already know this at least—with his great epic about Stepan Bagrov, *Notes about Hunting, Fishing, Childhood Years*, in all of which he appeared as a great and simple poet of nature; with his dying hand, he wrote a hymn to the emancipation of the centuries-old slavery of serfdom of a great people, beloved by him, with all the powers of his broad, sacred, and simple soul.[18]

Meanwhile, while dear to all of us during his life, and regarded as a venerable elder to be revered after his death, Aksakov was torn to shreds in an angry article by Vasily Ushakov.

But do me a divine favor, don't rush, you people of yesterday and those of today, to pronounce judgment on Vasily

16. "Suddenly" (Lat.).

17. Visyasha was a character in Ushakov's tale "Piyusha" (1835), intended as a caricature of Belinsky.

18. Aksakov's poem "At the News of the Impending Emancipation of the Serfs" (1858) was published in 1861.

Ushakov—and the main thing, don't think that he wrote that heated article out of hostility toward Sergei Aksakov or because of any literary envy—but do read, on the one hand, Aksakov's literary reminiscences, and remember, if only in general terms, according to the text book, what the merchant Nikolai Polevoy did, the significance of the *Moscow Telegraph*, and so on.

Striking emptiness of the content of life wafts from S. T. Aksakov's literary reminiscences—and it wafts precisely because this book is both so profoundly genuine, like everything he wrote, and genuinely talented, transporting you completely into the world that it depicts. . . . "What petty interests with enormous pretensions on literary aristocracy!" you think, as I do, too, being a man of that era, I think just as you do, whether reading about the way Prince Shakhovskoy, Zagoskin, Aksakov himself, Pisarev, and Kokoshkin spent their time at Kokoshkin's country house near Moscow; he was then director of the Moscow theater; or about the literary-theatrical aspirations of all these people of that time, so deserving of respect! For example, the late vaudevillian Pisarev occupies an enormous place in S. T. Aksakov's reminiscences. Perhaps he was a talented man by nature, but he wasted that talent on exactly the same nonsense as do Messrs. Rodislavsky and Dyachenko, the authors of vaudevilles with disguises. Perhaps, not even perhaps, but certainly, because we're always morally obliged to believe the honest narrator—his was a nature infuriatingly passionate and sensitive, and passion cut him down early; why, just look what this passion was consumed by! A man gives his life and his soul for the wings of a theater, not for the sake of dramatic art, but simply for the wings. The trouble is not in the fact that he loses his mind over some foolish young woman, and that she drives him to consumption—this sort of misfortune can happen to any decent man; but it is the fact that he was thoroughly steeped in the putrid air of theatrical wings, as only Mr. Rodislavsky or other figures of Russian dramaturgy can be; that he loved the nonsense of theatrical costumes as trumpery, ceruse, and rouge themselves, just as he loves ceruse and rouge *an sich.*[19] The trouble is that he becomes infuriated, a nervously infuriated man, principally for the actors or his own vulgar inventions, that he fulminates with his own witty couplets at a popular journalist-merchant with completely trivial views on life and the business of art—from the vilest points of view.

Remember that at this time, the popular merchant-publicist, not yet the author of the *Comedy about the Fedosya Sidorovna's War against the Chinese*, *Parasha the Siberian Woman*, *Yermak*, and so on,[20] but the eager and daring catcher of all the new tendencies of life, the keen-eyed watchman of progress, the destroyer of all routine, who had already written a story called "Simeon Kirdyap," a protest against the separatists and separation very daring for its time, and who expressed himself afterward with great energy in the novel *The Oath at the Lord's Sepulcher*, and in *The History of the Russian People*, which, no matter what you want to say, had an important, even positive meaning in many respects.[21]

I don't even consider it necessary to speak about the negative side: it was the beginning of the historical belching forth of localities, nationalities, and interpretations trampled underfoot by Karamzin so that he could glorify his own idea of the absolute state. I'm intentionally choosing these sides of Polevoy's activity, in order to show that he was not a Westernizer, but a man of the people, who knew the people as well as Pogodin did, and significantly better than Zagoskin, not to mention Prince Shakhovskoy, Pisarev with Kokoshkin, and perhaps even better than Aksakov himself. After all, some three years later, for example, *The Bigamist* appeared,[22] Shakhovskoy's attempt at writing a folk drama, and the popular merchant in a well-aimed, mean, and talented parody (which you can read in a celebrated book, namely, his *Literary Sketches*); it shattered its Ducray-Dumenil national

19. "In themselves" (Ger.).

20. Plays by Nikolai Polevoy, written in 1842, 1840, and 1845, respectively.

21. The play was written in 1832, the novel in 1829.

22. Published in 1836.

character, demolished it mercilessly, without paying attention to the fact that it, this drama, for the first time, touched living strains of folk life that had not been affected by anyone until then, even if it was done as a poor imitation, destroyed it in the name of an ideal, in the name of that very same national character, but one that he understood incomparably more broadly. Then, a few years later, that keen publicist boldly rises up against *The Hand of the Lord* in the name of that same ideal.

I maintain that Polevoy was not a Westernizer at all, and therefore it becomes even more complicated to understand the positions of the two sides. What kind of Westernizer would treasure every old document as a holy relic, every popular song, publishing them in his *Telegraph*, which in one of its columns, for example, displays Moscow to a visiting friend with fanatic love and with complete historical knowledge?

There's no point in talking about it as far as his activity as a hunter of all new tendencies of life. . . . Articles about Goethe, Byron, and other leading lights of contemporary literature of the time, acquainting readers with the fate of romance literature, the cult of Shakespeare, Dante, and others—translations from Hoffmann, critiques of everything new in young French literature, daring reverence for Hugo, and lastly, possible arguments about governmental structures in civilized countries that were finally allowed to appear, and these as strongly phrased as possible, even according to Cousin,[23] discussions of Kant, Fichte, Schelling, and Hegel; seizing upon every new, living idea, sympathy for every new manifestation in life and art, audacious enthusiasm for every new universal tendency—that's what the *Telegraph* was. It's no wonder that everything young and fresh was enchanted by it, at first the sensible young and fresh, and even that was not so sensible.Then the sensible part receded . . . but more about that later. I will take up the sword at a particular, given moment.

23. Victor Cousin (1792–1867) was a French philosopher who wrote on "the true, the beautiful, and the good."

What did its embittered enemies use first of all to oppose this vital tendency? The old men—Derzhavin's odes, Kheraskov's narrative poems, and Maksim Nevzorov's works. The popular leader worshipped "Bagrim's heir" even to excess, and later even wrote a long article full of nonsense about Shchukin's edition of the works of the poet of "Felitsa," and Merzlyakov amused himself with Kheraskov, while the younger generation was disgusted by "the morality of Maksim Nevzorov."[24] The flesh-colored stockings kept busy with "Poor Liza," and "Natalya, the Boyar's Daughter;" but, in the first place, the younger generation knew all too well that "Liza's pond" behind the Simonov Monastery, wasn't really "Liza's pond [*Lizin prud*]," but "Fox pond [*Lisiy prud*]"; besides, what did it care about "Poor Liza" when it was greedily intoxicated with the tales of the fashionable young writer Bestuzhev-Marlinsky in the *Telegraph*, who was surrounded by the double halo—talent and a tragic fate? What did it care about the "moans of a gray dove,"[25] sung by His Excellency I. I. Dmitriyev when almost every week the *Moscow News* published in its announcement of forthcoming books notice of a new poem by Pushkin or Baratynsky, various almanacs, where these glorious, or not so glorious names appeared again, but still names beloved by the younger generation. Of course, the youth of that time didn't fling itself only at *The Northern Flowers*, and didn't copy only *The Polar Star* into its secret notebooks; but it devoured any kind of carrion like *Cepheids*, *The Garland*, or, as the publisher himself joked in the preface, *The Graces' Broom*.[26] And this is completely understandable. In some unfortunate *Broom*, it would encounter one of the excellent tales by Thomas Moore in

24. Polevoy's preface to an edition of Derzhavin's *Works* (1845), previously published in the *Telegraph* (1832). Maksim Nevzorov (1762–1827) was a minor Russian poet.

25. Ivan Dmitriyev (1760–1837) was a Russian statesman and poet associated with the sentimentalist movement in Russian literature. The reference is to his popular song, "Moans the Gray Dove" (1792).

26. Names of almanacs published in the 1820s.

"Lalla Rookh," the patron saint of Khorosan, or some sufficient translation from Goethe and Schiller, or from Lamartine and Hugo. . . . But you were not treated to *The Rossiada.*[27]

But the old men in buskins and those in flesh-colored stockings grew angry, completely lost their tempers and both in the *European Herald* and in the gentle *Galatea*, and in the even gentler *Ladies' Journal* of Prince Shalikov, and it goes without saying, as it has been forever, that they lost out.

In the final analysis, what could the narrow circle around Aksakov or the broader, stronger one gathering around the *Moscow Herald*—what could they do to oppose the vital tendency in the *Telegraph*? It's true that this last circle didn't rise up against the great phenomenon in Russian literature, against Pushkin, and was in contact with that brilliant planet's satellites, but it didn't outdo the *Telegraph* in bowing down to the common idol also in other respects; in its embittered enmity and struggle with Polevoy, it tried, on the contrary, to outdo the old men in buskins and even the *European Herald* with its vulgar cynicism of its articles about *The History of the Russian People.*

The *Moscow Herald* suffered from the beginning with an unfortunate identification with the old rubbish and rags that later cut off all the shoots of life in the *Muscovite* of the 1850s. . . . If you wrote an article on contemporary literature, let's say, for example, about the lyric poets—and all of a sudden you saw to your astonishment and horror that alongside the names of Pushkin, Lermontov, Koltsov, Khomyakov, Ograev, Fet, Polonsky, and Mey that appeared in it, were the names of Countess Rostopchina, Mrs. Karolina Pavlova, Mr. M. Dmitriyev, and Mr. Fedotov—and, oh, horror! Avdotya Glinka had even squeezed in. You see it, and you can't believe your own eyes! It seems that you saw both the final proof and even the page proof, and

27. "Lalla Rookh" is an Oriental romance by the Irish poet Thomas Moore (1779–1852), published in 1817. *The Rossiada* is an epic poem (1771–1779) by Mikhail Kheraskov, based on the capture of Kazan (1552) by Ivan the Terrible.

suddenly, as if by a wave of the magic wand, unbidden guests' names appear in print! Or else, the young editors watch—sharply and suspiciously—lest some elegy by Mr. Dmitriyev or some old sin of an equally famous literary figure slipped through into an issue of the journal. If your vigilance were relaxed in the slightest, Mr. Dmitriyev would be present, and Mrs. Pavlova would construct something, and finally, to the overwhelming despair of the young editors, the primary place in the journal would be occupied by some inquisitorial article by Mr. Strudza, or one of Mr. Kulzhinsky's stories from last year would adorn the literary section![28] And this all occurred in the 1850s, just as it did in the 1830s.

But the main thing is that in the 1850s, the nationalist movement already had Mr. Ostrovsky, while Slavophilism had begun to manifest itself very energetically, honestly attempting to rupture the association with Messrs. Kulzhinsky, Muravyov, and other knights, yet none of this had existed in the 1830s. There was only a profound article on literature by Ivan Kireyevsky, even profound by any standards, published in the *Dawn*, not only in terms of those years, but for any year, two or three poems by Khomyakov, two or three original and talented stories by Pogodin, although, as was his habit, they were finished sloppily, as well as his and Shevyryov's professorial activity, limited more or less to the confines of the auditorium, and Aksakov, the only genuine artist to emerge from this circle, who was devoted then to absolute nonsense. Another man, although original, but really talented, even belonging to a narrow theatrical circle, rather than to that of the *Moscow Herald*, and who, moreover, spent his whole life associating with obscurantists, with the Petersburg Slavophilism that derived, incidentally, from a completely honorable man, Admiral Shishkov; Zagoskin had not yet pub-

28. Alexander Strudza (1791–1854) was a Russian diplomat, statesman, and minor poet. Ivan Kulzhinsky (1803–1884) was a professor, journalist, and writer of the period.

lished his *Yury Miloslavsky*,[29] and was known only as the author of comedies belonging to the category of contrived works that the younger generation justifiably rejected.

But even after the appearance of the celebrated *Yury Miloslavsky*—was there really any sort of revolution in literary conceptions? Polevoy rendered justice to the attempt—quite talented for that time—even from today's point of view, treating it without the required ruthlessness. Meanwhile, he himself with his understanding of the Russian people and its history, stood incomparably higher than the first Russian novelist, and young people felt this very clearly. After all, it was only later, and artificially besides, that Polevoy attained in his dramas the artificially sweet banality that prevails in Zagoskin's novels in general. At that time, in the 1830s, he was highly regarded.

Have you, people of the latest generation, read his literary confession, written as a preface to Polevoy's *Outline of Russian Literature*?[30] Not too long ago, only about two years, I was rereading it—and a feeling of tender sympathy to this talented individual, so eager for light, completely self-made—moved my soul—and how extremely despicable, I thought, was the famous parody of Zhukovsky's ballad "Svetlana," composed by one of the untalented, but well-respected old-timers, in which Polevoy is accused before some sort of tribunal (old-timers can't live without tribunals), among other things of:

> . . . everyone knows
> That even in Kursk he was
> An old friend of Shakespeare's,
> When he murdered his friend
> For three hundred rubles,
> And then dissected him
> In the Bolshoy Theater.

29. Mikhail Zagoskin's historical tragedy *Yury Miloslavsky* was published in 1829.
30. *Outline of Russian Literature* was published in 1839.

But in the end it states spitefully about the poor, talented publicist, who was overcome by fate, driven by circumstances, that he achieved a great deal, and now . . .

> Lives with a hack journalist
> At his expense.

I won't even mention that in the Bolshoy Theater *Hamlet* was dissected by the greatest scenic genius of the Russian stage, that is, Mochalov, and that Polevoy, in his poetic translation of *Hamlet*,[31] the only one possible for our Russian stage, murdered his old friend in such a way that the play almost dissolved into proverbs. But that still doesn't mean anything because there's no quarreling about taste; but to abuse a man, who struggled for a long time, honestly, fervently, and who was constrained by the force of completely external circumstances to veer sharply from one road to another, forced to rescue his family from hunger, and because he didn't edit his own journal, to work for Senkovsky, to abuse, instead of regretting this weakness of character in a talented literary man, is worthy only of those old-timers who, attaching their substance to the nationalist movement, corroded the purity of the endeavors of the *Moscow Herald* and the *Muscovite* like rust. . . . (the *Russian Discourse* and also the *Day* weren't tarnished by their association—and thank God for that!).

Oh, old-timers, old-timers! Many years have passed since we, that is, the circle at the head of which Pogodin and Ostrovsky stood, offered our best efforts and best forces of life with all the vigor and energy of youth, with its sparkle and freshness, to the service of the nationalist movement, yet still couldn't establish our journalistic organ only because the editor in chief Pogodin was incapable of renouncing destructive associations; after this almost ten years passed, but I still can't help remembering our vain, though fervent attempts without a surge of indignation. . . .

31. Polevoy's translation of *Hamlet* was published in 1837.

There are, I repeat, new books in which either an entire literary epoch or a particular tendency is manifested without ceremony. M. Dmitriyev's *Moscow Elegies*,[32] for example, is such a book. It's short, but instructive, I can tell you, capable of driving the most genuine Muscovite, if only there's not much of the real Muscovite essence in him, into a complete fury with the Moscow that's presented as an ideal of the "venerable" bard, to employ the high style. It's the sort of book that will make it possible, if, contrary to expectation, so much as a single copy remains intact for distant posterity together with our denunciatory publications—to justify even the crude hatred for one's native soil and for the Moscow of some "Denunciatory *Brand*," like Mr. Askochensky, "*Instructive Brand*,"[33] should it, too, remain intact, a book that will make it possible to justify our little adherents of Büchner's and Moleschott's materialist ideas. It's not possible to perpetrate a greater infamy on Moscow than what these poetic trifles have done; the most dedicated enemy couldn't conceive of anything like this. . . . Those aren't Famusov-Zagoskin's good-hearted stories about the charms of the old gentry way of life, with a crowd of loyal servants, nor are they the comic delights of fools' and clowns' buffoonery, nor the naive enthusiasms, which, after all, unmask themselves . . . no! This is Famusov, who attains lyric intoxication, pride, and madness on a very strange topic, namely, that Arcadia is only possible under two formulas: nobility on the one hand, and obstinacy on the other; that is Famusov, openly and intentionally despising the folk among both the merchants and the rural emancipated class, Famusov-the-idealist, who shamelessly regrets that in order to depict zephyrs and cupids, they don't carry away . . .

32. Dmitriyev's *Moscow Elegies* was published in 1858.

33. Viktor Askochensky (1813–79) was a Russian writer, journalist and historian of Orthodoxy in Ukraine. This is an attempt to render an untranslatable pun in Russian.

. . . on many wagons
Children ripped from their mothers and fathers,

and who sees in old Moscow the ideal of a gentry city . . . in the great, historical, and national Moscow, freely, organically developing in the course of centuries with its "suburbs," vainly contained by its white walls, then its earthen city walls, straining to expand into the limitless distance.

Even people with a broader ideal of nationalism, and all the old-timers of the 1830s, either wearing buskins or flesh-colored stockings, had precisely that limited ideal in their souls, and lacked the strength to do battle with the popular merchant class. . . . Even serious, nationalist people belonging to the circle of the *Moscow Herald* couldn't fight with it, because in essence they didn't know what they were fighting for. . . . They inclined toward tradition, history, and the people and, of course, he was attracted to the very same things by his inclinations, only they didn't distinguish the traditions of the people from those of the old-timers, and proclaimed their solidarity with them, which he,

A measuring stick, broken into pieces,
An offshoot of the Kokoshkin merchant clan,[34]

couldn't share with them, for being a democrat by birth and spirit, he hated the old-timers' legends just as strongly as Griboyedov did, who was an aristocrat by birth.

Everything was in his favor, every new European idea, which he grasped quickly and communicated at once to his readers; every tendency of contemporary life, including the appropriate feeling of nationalism itself. For a while that feeling had to be completely negative toward the artistic structure of our historical existence that was created by Karamzin according to

34. The beginning of an anonymous epigram on Polevoy; its conclusion is: "What sort of *Son of the Fatherland* are you?—You're just a son of a bitch."

one concept of absolute government—and Polevoy became the representative in his *History* and in his novels of that negative necessity: he started the work, which is still unfinished, and won't be completed in the near future.

Could the abuse of the two *Heralds*, M. Dmitriyev's epigrams, and Pisarev's vaudevillian couplets really wound him at that time? All of that was incomparably beneath his level.

It is perfectly clear that impressionable people like V. A. Ushakov (I'm once more returning to the point where I started) were on his side, and his total supporters; they boldly attacked everything that was hostile to him and to them, and no matter what, for example, your and my profound respect for the late Aksakov, Ushakov's column ceases to arouse feelings. . . . Why even in less important issues than those I have broached, in depicting the general mood of the era, Polevoy and his tendency have constantly parted ways with his opponents.

There was, for example, or better to say, there only began to be at this time an extremely strange eccentric on the stage, whose name I mentioned and whose name I constantly introduce in the most daring manner into the history of one entire aspect of our development, not merely as the name of a scenic artist, a man who implemented images created by literature, but as the name of a representative of a tendency, the independent creator of images, a poet who in his creation was more solid and sublime than his dramatists. I'm speaking, of course, of Mochalov,[35] but not so that we start talking about him. There will be space for him, one of the greatest educators of our entire generation, in the future course of these notes. Here I will touch only on how one side and the other related to this towering genius. Aksakov, for example, as an artist himself, and Zagoskin, as a talented and impressionable Russian, Prince Shakhovskoy and Kokoshkin, as great experts and admirers of the theater; some were the only ones, of course, like Aksakov, both understood and felt (others merely felt)—what sort

35. Pavel Mochalov (1800–1888) was a famous Russian actor.

of a powerful and original force he was, but either all of them, with the sole exception of the effeminate and impressionable Zagoskin, accepted him as he has been created by God; everyone wanted something conventional in art from him, something conventional in life, too, and couldn't be reconciled with his debauchery, were disturbed by his plebianism, and so forth. Only Polevoy was destined to accept him as he was, who crowned him with the role of Hamlet, also Belinsky, who interpreted the originality of Mochalov's Hamlet. But we'll explain all this later.

I've told you, my male readers (I count on few female readers of these chapters and assume that the so-called serious ones among them have more taste for anatomical, rather than historical dissertations), about the position of the literary factions at the moment I've chosen.

But please don't rush to take sides completely, not only with the columnist Ushakov against S. T. Aksakov and his circle, but even on the side of Polevoy against the old-timers and the *Moscow Herald.* Please remember and constantly keep in mind the proverb "Look before you leap," and keep the ends in mind, namely:

1. that Ushakov will finish by writing "Vysasha";
2. that Polevoy will write "Parasha," "Yermak," and so forth;
3. that in the end, the battle he waged against Karamzin's idea of absolute government will end in our day with the Ukrainian joke about Russian history, placing the Muscovite state on the same level as various weakening khanates and so forth, either with maritime hallucinations, or simply with mortal hallucinations of Russian historians,[36] in the journal the *Spark.*

Keep all that in mind; and since the process of literary movements is an organic one, see if it doesn't already contain the beginning of the plan of decomposition.

36. Another untranslatable Russian pun—maritime and mortal.

It is there, undoubtedly. So far I have spoken in the wolf's language; now it's time to speak "against the wolf."

Polevoy and his movement really did reflect all contemporary tendencies as if in a mirror, but they did so uniformly, superficially, almost unconsciously. The younger generation, brought up on these unconsciously reflected tendencies, was divided into two parts: one, the minority, who went to the heart of the matter, took the tendency seriously, transferred them into real life, and soon felt a terrible dissatisfaction with superficial reflections; while the other, a more numerous one, of course, was completely satisfied with the upper crust, and probably to this day continues to live its life in uniform worship of both Hugo and Bestuzhev-Marlinsky, in total incomprehension of anything new and vital, beginning with Gogol.

Both groups of the younger generation are two phases of what I have already called Russian Romanticism and what's totally different from other romanticisms. Russian Romanticism differs so much from other foreign versions in that it accepts every idea, no matter how wild or absurd, and takes it to the extreme, and besides, puts it into practice. A German, for example, can derive the human species from monkeys, and serve in any capacity you wish, including that of a pastor: he can reach the extreme negation of all moral principles or else the most phantasmagoric hallucinations and will not go to seed, because eccentrics such as Hoffmann, who could find serenity in his princes-leeches, Serpentinas, and other creatures of his bewitching imagination, only in Auerbach's cellar,[37] and indeed created most of them there, or like Max Stirner, who took the idea of the absolute rights of the human "I" to the extreme, insane consistency, and was confined in an insane asylum, are very few. The great Hegel, according to the testimony of the well-known Heine, expressed himself disrespectfully in a discussion concerning

37. "Serpentinas" are characters in short stories by E. T. A. Hoffmann. Auerbach's was the name of a tavern in Berlin.

the heavenly planets, and then sat down calmly to play a game of whist. The Frenchman, too, with the exception of feverish periods of history, when the dear *tigre-singe*, is carried away to the point of dizziness, and is in general extremely inclined to a *moral* life, to enjoyment of fantastic and other delights, according to the completely reliable reports of Fyodor Dostoevsky.[38] But we are a somewhat irrepressible nation, somewhat crudely primitive people. With us an idea can't simply be separated from life. Once our head is set spinning by a certain tendency, it really starts to twirl. We have offered sad sacrifices to the whirlwind in the form of Polezhayevs, Mochalovs, Bestuzhev-Marlinskys, and even Lermontovs.

People of that purely Russian cast, people with a serious thirst for ideas and life, capable of burning the candle at both ends or staking life on any card, and, in addition, except also for a small circle of sensible people, capable of starting something intentionally, were barely satisfied with the tendency of the *Telegraph* and the general level of literature at that time. Lounging, Epicurism, and besides, those rather cheap phrases—moon, dream, maiden—rubbish, rubbish in Senkovsky-Brambeus's recent clever expression,[39] preached in the poetry of Pushkin's satellites and all sorts of other rhymesters in innumerable almanacs; German sentimentalism, which soon began to be mixed in Polevoy's and others' tales, with the feverishly agitating tendency, and led in a completely consistent way to the well-known, feigned vulgar epilogue of *Abbadonna*—all that could completely satisfy only those young people,[40] who, like my tutor, in essence translated romantic aspirations into the substance of the famous song:

38. "Tiger-monkey" (French) was a widely used phrase of Voltaire's; Pushkin wrote an early work in which he described a Frenchman as a combination of a tiger and a monkey. The Dostoevsky reference is to his *Winter Notes on Summer Impressions* (1863), chapters v–viii.

39. This expression has not been located in Senkovsky's works.

40. Polevoy's novel *Abbadonna* was published in 1834.

For love alone did nature
Bring us into this world;[41]

and young women of the provinces or Zamoskvorechye, who kept expecting Lensky to reappear alive in the last chapter of Pushkin's *Eugene Onegin*, and be reunited with his widowed Olga, just as Onegin would be with Tatyana. From the youth who believed in the song mentioned above, there emerged either tippling clerks or bribe-taking doctors, or simply crybabies and drunkards; from the young women, of course, came Kukushkinas, who, even in their later years, eagerly read "when obstacles are eliminated and the two loving souls are joined."[42] All this is as it should be. Even many of the poets of that day, cursing life and lamenting how difficult it was

. . . to be in a crowd of unfeeling people,[43]

served calmly until they attained a high rank and a badge for twenty-five years of service.

All of this was not only completely satisfied with Polevoy and his movement, but, probably, if it still thrives, is still being satisfied even today. And not even probably, but certainly. Have you read, for example, Mr. Zhandr's recently published poem "Society"?[44] An amusing incident. The 1830s, just as they were, suddenly spring up before your eyes in a belated appearance—just as they really were, with unacknowledged poets and otherworldly countesses and princesses, with speeches *à la* Bestuzhev-Marlinsky, and with the entire male sex dressed in frock coats with wide lapels and the lowest waists, with shoes and open-work stockings,

41. The source is unknown.

42. An inexact quotation from Kukushkina's tirade in Ostrovsky's play *A Profitable Position* (1857).

43. The source is unknown.

44. Andrey Zhandr (1789–1873). The full title is "Society: A Novel of a Past Epoch in Verse" (1830).

emerging from under their tight-fitting trousers; the feminine or gentler sex wearing hats with some sort of little seashells, with enormous puffed sleeves, and high waists in contrast. . . . Or take a peek into the backyards of literature, read *Natasha Podgorich* or other recent novels, which the esteemed Moscow novelist Mr. Voskresensky continues to present to his public.[45] There you have the mummified remains of Polevoy and his movement.

Their extremely fruitless future lay in themselves, that is, in Polevoy and in the literary movement of that time, who is passionate and talented [a footnote in the Russian edition says Grigoryev made an error]. The literature of the end of the 1830s had already turned into the most vulgar almanacs. Pushkin had already begun to turn away and to withdraw into himself. Polevoy was already offering his hand to Bulgarin and could no longer understand Pushkin. And it would have been difficult for him, after being raised on Bulgarin's novel *Ivan Vyzhigin* and condescendingly treating his famous novel, *Dmitry the Pretender*,[46] to understand scenes from *Boris Godunov*, which appeared, though infrequently in good almanacs.

It was Pushkin's *Boris* that became in its majestic unity for many people, including Polevoy, a stumbling block and a temptation. On the other hand, the same Boris clearly forced another literary man, who was fated to answer the needs of serious young people, to lay the foundation for the future of critical consciousness, and besides, to raise and provide to that generation its real leader, Vissarion Belinsky.

The godfather of the great fighter was the cynic-seminarian Nikodim Nadoumko.[47] That is, it was Nikodim Nadoumko until

45. The novel *Natasha Podgorich* was published in 1858 by Mikhail Voskresensky (1803–1867), a Russian poet, writer, and translator.

46. Faddei Bulgarin (1789–1859) was a Russian writer, journalist, and publisher of Polish ancestry. In addition to his newspaper work, he rejuvenated the Russian novel in his satirical work *Ivan Vyzhigin* (1829).

47. A pen name for Nikolai Nadezhdin (1804–1856), who made his critical name not as Nadezhdin, but as the "Ex-Student Nikodim Nadoumko."

1831 and only in the first issue of the *Telescope*, which was newly conceived in that year. Then N. I. Nadezhdin, the journal's editor appeared, one of the most original minds in Russia, and one of enormous erudition, but with an absence of character, equal to that of another contemporary, Senkovsky, equally original in mind, and also possessing an astonishing erudition.

In 1829, when the *European Herald*, decrepit to a state "akin to pity," casting sleep or misery, both with its ancient Luzhnitsky and its literary views,[48]

> Of Ochakov's time and the conquest of Crimea,[49]

a new, fresh, cynically nasty, but in its own way, witty and unquestionably energetic man named Nikodim Nadoumko appeared in an article, "A Swarm of Nihilists." The word "nihilist" didn't have the same meaning for him that Turgenev later gave it in our day.[50] He simply referred to people who know *nothing* as nihilists, who have no basis in art and life, while our nihilists know five little books and base themselves on them.[51] Nadoumko started conversations that were strange in form and content with women who baked the communion bread, and with proofreaders, and other characters brought in by him about the emptiness of the literary movement, mercilessly took up arms, though more to satisfy the elders, against Pushkin, though no one sympathized with him, and against Polevoy for his superficiality and rambling thoughts and feelings, with which many people sympathized. . . .

Then, after achieving fame for himself with a series of articles under the pseudonym of Nadoumko, and having attained

---

48. The pen name of the editor of the *European Herald* Mikhail Kachenovsky (1775–1842).

49. A quotation from Chatsky's monologue in act 2, scene 5 of Griboyedov's verse comedy *Woe from Wit*.

50. Ivan Turgenev in his *Fathers and Children* (1862).

51. An ironic reference to the works of Büchner, Moleschott, and others.

a doctoral degree and a professorship for his dissertation, "De poësia romantica,"[52] Nadezhdin parted from the elders and their journal and began to publish the *Telescope.* In the first issue, as I mentioned, he alone of all the critics of that time, declared himself for Pushkin's *Boris*, and took the role of the leader of the entire serious part of the younger generation.

But this relates to the year 1831.

52. "About Romantic Poetry" (Lat.).

VI

Echoes of the Past

In the meantime the old generation, leaving the field of action, or obliged to do so by the immutable laws of history, lived out its life somehow, and maintained in itself the traces of those tendencies, which, at that time, it carried away with them more or less powerfully, and did transmit or attempt to transmit those tendencies, which were still fundamental to it, to the younger generation.

Of course, that was the case. No matter how few ideas of a serious nature my father took away from his youth, he still remembered, thanks to traditions, and:

> I sing of Russia, freed from the barbarians,
> The crushing of the Tatar power and their oppressed pride.[1]

Then:

1. The first lines of Kheraskov's heroic poem *The Rossiada* (1779).

Russian princes, boyars, commanders,
Going beyond the Don to seek freedom.[2]

As well as other tirades from *Dmitry Donskoy*, together, naturally, with the parody *Mityukha Valdajsky*, and another one, in which the reply to the khan's emissary was expressed with great energy:

Go and tell Mamai,
That I'll . . . him, etc.[3]

He recalled and read, naturally, with enthusiasm in a manner, warmed by tradition, both Derzhavin's ode "God" and "Felitsa." However, he was already a man not of Derzhavin's ilk, but of Karamzin's era; he didn't know Sumarokov at all, left Kheraskov in peace, strictly speaking, however, he cited Neledinsky-Meletsky and Dmitriyev with great feeling,[4] especially:

Ah, if I had known earlier
That love brings trouble to the world.[5]

Incidentally, he parodied the end of that tender poem in a cynical manner.

My father was a strange man in many respects; rather, he could be strange in different epochs. This doesn't include his purely everyday attitudes. . . . But from the spiritual point of view, he represented precisely the type of an intelligent, ordinary person of the early Karamzinian period. In order to represent that type, fate bestowed on him sufficient sensitivity, the ease of assimilating impressions, insufficient moral rigidity, and intellectual depth. Just as in life he was capable of submitting to

2. The first lines of Ozerov's tragedy *Dmitry Donskoy* (1807).
3. From a parody of Ozerov's tragedy written by P. N. Semenov (1810).
4. Yury Neledinsky-Meletsky (1751–1828) was a soldier, senator, and secretary of state of the Russian Empire and a minor poet.
5. From a poem by Dmitriyev written in 1792.

any circumstance for the sake of peace and quiet, and he did so in his spiritual development as well. But in reality that submission was merely seeming, purely external. Something stubbornly remained in him for those who knew him as well as I came to afterward. During the 1850s, for example, he was already past sixty, but, when he suddenly became a widower, and was immediately surrounded by a circle of young people, he accommodated to his new situation very easily, finding it amusing; not only did he not interfere with all of us, but in the most naive way he shared our literary interests. . . . But in reality, that naiveté wasn't sincere. "Something," I repeat, stubbornly took hold of him, and at times it would burst into the open, especially at the least unfavorable circumstance. . . . In general, fate treated him unkindly, as it did all our clan, and alas! One of its least kind gifts to the old man was, of course, myself. So long as things went well, one can say, he followed me everywhere, but when the good, or at least, the bearable way of life changed and became unbearable, the old man again would sink into his stubborn egoism.

This same something also had a hold on him in the intellectual-moral world. It wasn't his individuality or personality, because he didn't have a personality to speak of, and it developed somehow that he didn't value either his own or other people's personality—but something, if it wasn't knocked into him (because, as far as I know, grandfather didn't beat him, and even forgave a great deal to the good-natured child, who probably was whiny), at least crushing him with his oppression, destroying any serious sort of receptivity in him. And this something was not his father's, my grandfather's convictions, because the latter had firm convictions, but simply—it was the entire former epoch, accepted by his soul indifferently, unconsciously, so to say, slavishly, without any logical consideration taking hold of his mind in this common chaos. That grandfather, as I've already said, was like Stepan Bagrov,[6] although, of course, less

6. The protagonist in Aksakov's *Family Chronicle* (1856).

grandiose and less grandiosely placed in his life circumstances; he was responsible for the development of such impressionability in my father, of that there is no doubt whatsoever. He frightened him from childhood, so much so that my father never felt any love for him, but felt only fear; from his earliest years he feared reasoning more than anything, and became accustomed to accepting everything indiscriminately. Later in life, as soon as he was given a little freedom, he "went astray," naturally, he fell into rather lowly situations, and was forced to settle in it and, naturally, submit to it. But human nature is made in such a way that even with the weakest start in life, it still stubbornly yearns for independence and to express that independence in reality; once unleashed, it expresses itself in reality not as independence, but as petty tyranny. Slaves inevitably become despots at the least opportunity: their despotism is not a manifestation of their personality, but the involuntary imitation of the despotism of their former masters. In life—at the slightest sign of good and comfortable circumstances—father definitely imitated grandfather's despotism, but of course, in the absence of firm inclinations in his nature, this manifestation never contained a drop of seriousness, but almost always ended comically.

But it is exactly for this reason that my father is particularly valuable as an object of study, because he was an intelligent and also morally active man, completely along the lines of someone one might find by reading *A Student's Diary*. It wasn't in vain that he maintained a relationship with the author of that work, the late Zhikharev, longer than with other comrades in the university boarding school, although Stepan Petrovich attained a high rank, while he remained a titular counselor all his life. . . .

I have touched upon all these general bases in my father's nature merely to explain by which intellectual and literary tendencies *he* must have lived.

He respected Derzhavin, just as he venerated various fetishes, the only difference being that he wasn't afraid of him.

He recited several of his odes with a particular kind of declamation, with an almost tearful voice, and didn't allow himself to write indecent parodies, although he had a great passion for producing them (which I also inherited). . . . But, to be accurate, that was a blind and unconscious fetish. Karamzin, in his early works, Dmitriyev in his tales, and Neledinsky-Meletsky in his sentimental songs, were altogether different matters for him: he, too, of course, once *loved* and felt *tender* in his own way toward these songs, if he was capable of loving and feeling tender. . . . Dmitriyev's tales were his *profession de foi* of a half-modest, half-moral view of life relations of his time;[7] Karamzin in his earliest works tried very hard to develop goodness and kindness of heart, qualities that were most useful for living life in peace and quiet. . . . The veneration of Karamzin as the historian of the Russian state was, however, both blind and insincere again, like fetishism, and in particular was founded on the historiographer's high rank and his proximity to the royal court.

Zhukovsky somehow passed by my father, without touching his soul in any way. That's completely understandable. My father was an entirely ordinary, carnal man: he found transcendent aspirations and transcendent lyricism totally incomprehensible. As an intelligent man, he couldn't fail to appreciate Pushkin's genius, but his attitude to Pushkin was somehow very strange. At times he would judge him as a lewd writer, and, as he used to say, an evil one—all this, of course, as opposed to Karamzin, whose every page throbbed with kindness; at other times, when members of the younger generation would begin to recite lines from Polezhayev, for example, he would say—"No! That's not Pushkin!" The next day he would go to a bookseller whom he knew in "town," (that is, the Arcade); he would bring any one of Pushkin's poems and recite it with great enthusiasm, even if it was with the old-fashioned style of declamation. He considered

7. "Profession of faith" (Fr.).

Griboyedov and the author of the *Dumy* and *Voynarovsky*,[8] as evil, but extremely talented writers, almost placing his range higher than Pushkin's. He felt very little sympathy for Bestuzhev-Marlinsky, someone the younger generation adored.

All of that, both the old and the new, was floating in the air around me, was read aloud past midnight by my father and Sergei Ivanovich in my parents' bedroom, next to mine; it was read indiscriminately, without differentiation. Both Pushkin and Marlinsky, *The History of the Russian State*, *Ivan Vyzhigin*, *Yury Miloslavsky*, and the novels of Sir Walter Scott, which at that time constantly appeared in translations from the French.

The reading continued avidly. However, the novels of Radcliffe, de Genlis, Ducray-Duminil, and August von Lafontaine were read with special zest, sweetness, sincere sympathy, and eagerness.[9]

I consider it necessary to speak about them—and about the world with which they filled my childhood imagination, in a separate chapter.

---

8. Works by Kondraty Ryleyev (1795–1826), a Russian poet, publisher, and a leader of the Decembrist Revolt.
9. Madame de Genlis (1746–1830) was a French writer of the late eighteenth and early nineteenth centuries, known for her novels and theories of children's education.

VII

Belated Currents

Besides these living tendencies, carried by the air of life surrounding me—speaking literally, not metaphorically, around my childhood bed, there came the rustling sound of other impressions of a former time, now past. . . . Strictly speaking, these impressions were barely considered outdated, not completely replaced, and just somewhat obscured by new answers to the new demands of life, which still continued to act, influence, and edify. . . . Perhaps they belonged to the kind of impressions whose effect on the soul is unwillingly admitted by the young, fresh generations, but which still burdened them as an unavoidable heritage, ensconced in them as a whole organic world that could not be separated from the soul.

As I have already said, that was the world of the old—and it goes without saying, translated novels, by means of which many-sided, more or less belated tendencies of former times, flooded into the new waves of life.

My childhood room was alongside my parents' room, and my little bed stood next to the door, so that my father's old-fashioned emotional reading, and Sergei Ivanovich's sentimental reading—deacon-like and droning—were perfectly audible to me during the night, in addition to the fact that no one prevented me from listening in some corner to the reading, which usually started after five o'clock, that is, after the end of evening tea in my room, where the whole family took its tea. Only rarely would my father notice, and then only pro forma (as he would say about various official proceedings), "you'd better go into the hall and play with Marishka," that is, with Marina, a little girl my own age, brought intentionally from the village of Vladimir for the young master's pleasure; but my father didn't worry about having his directions fulfilled without fail, since he himself was too engrossed in the reading; it was only if something too terrible or scandalous was clearly foreseen in the book that he would send me away with the authority of parental power. And there were even means to do that. Only if it wasn't a summer evening, that is, if *nolens-volens*,[1] I wasn't obliged to go off to the garden or the courtyard; with a sinking heart I would tiptoe into the maid's room, which was located next to mine, and sit down next to Lukeriya, who was sewing by the door; not bothering her with conversation, I would place my ear against the door and, with just a small interruption, I would listen word for word to the very end of the horrors and scandals that were so enticing due to their secrecy. . . . Well, in the summer there was another means. I always noted carefully where my father placed the book that was being read: like the orderly man he was, he would always hide it in the same spot, on the top of the bureau, on the left side under the calendar. Then, the next morning, after Sergei Ivanovich left for the university, when I was supposed to be memorizing a short catechism, or the exceptions to the third Latin declension, or Schröckh's magnificent tales of Babylonian and Assyrian kings,[2] I would seize the moment

1. "Willingly-unwillingly" (Lat.).
2. Johann Matthias Shröckh's popular *Universal History for Study by Young People* (1787) was translated into Russian and reprinted frequently.

when my mother, in a cloying mood, was beginning to nag, pester, and bother Lukeriya, or, in a good mood, when she would begin to rearrange clothes and linens in her dressers, chatting serenely with the same much-hated and simultaneously loved Lukeriya—I would steal the book and, keeping Lebedev's Latin grammar handy and ready to hide it, I would devour the parts I hadn't heard or else reread the parts that I had, or else I would read ahead. If my mother approached and was in a bad mood, either to scold me or to comb my hair harshly, or if she was in a good mood—to show me affection and offer me coffee, as if nothing were wrong, I would cover the forbidden book with the work of the respected professor, and begin to repeat aloud the declension of *iter, itineris*, or repeat "the Creator is seen by His works and is always more perfect than His works," and so on. Then, making use of my mother's exit to the servants' room, I would bound into their bedroom with the swiftness of a gazelle, and place the book in its usual spot. When Sergei Ivanovych would return and demand a report of my morning's activities, I still wouldn't know the exceptions to the third declension, but would state with unaffected insolence that I had been sitting there all morning and that my mother could serve as my witness.

Moreover, I repeat that my father had recourse to such banishment pro forma (as he would say about various official matters), so that his conscience wouldn't reproach him and his parental responsibility would be fulfilled to some extent—while he himself, based on his own recollections from adolescence, and being a very smart, practical man, was profoundly convinced that such prohibitions were useless. . . . I could have become more and more convinced of this, especially later, when I had grown up, if only I'd regarded things more simply. He turned a blind eye to everything and evidently wanted to. . . . Well, if something was achieved against his will or without his knowledge, he would undertake such things pro forma and put "l'ascendant" to use. It's a pity that I recognized these traits with full clarity only when I no longer had any need for them. In general,

I would have spared myself many moral torments if I'd reacted more "naturally" to the affairs of this world. . . . The question is only whether, raised under such tendencies, which I've had the honor of describing to you with precision and detail, and accepting them entirely in earnest—whether I was even capable of understanding natural behavior in the affairs of this world. There were no living people before me for a long time, a very long time, only images from novels or from history. I had to achieve a somewhat natural attitude to life and to people with labor incomparably more persistent than that mental process necessary to apprehend the abstractions of Hegel's *Phenomenology of Spirit.* That somewhat more natural attitude was subsequently acquired with heartbreak and wounded pride!

Nevertheless, it would be dishonest to the highest degree to blame both the tendencies of the age—undermining in me a natural attitude toward life—and my father, who concerned himself very little with pruning the early and irregular shoots of the plant, which was growing before his very eyes. I am of the opinion—and at the age of forty-two, I hope that I might have the nerve to maintain it—that if you prune the offshoots of life's forces in one direction, they will grow in another. If a reflective life hadn't developed in me with terrible force, a life of animal passions would have developed with the same force, and it's really very difficult to say which is better. It seems my father understood this instinctively, and as a genuinely sensitive man, didn't attach much meaning to the spiritual life. In this, and in his beloved saying, "It'll all come out in the wash," he was wrong, of course, and later, when even in a man of thirty, the intellectual ferment "didn't come out in the wash," he could have convinced himself of his error at a glance; in any case, I consider him completely, although also instinctively, correct for not having recourse to oppressive and prohibitory measures.

I shall tell you one of my recent experiments in this regard, although my friends have already begun to chide me for my outrageous insertions and digressions. I happened to become the tutor of an extremely lazy and talented young man—jointly with an extremely serious English tutor, the most honest and limited gentleman of the bourgeoisie whom I have ever met in my life. Our methods of educating the youth were diametrically opposed. I wasn't a tutor, and to tell the truth, I would never supervise a puppy dog, let alone a young man; but in this case I undertook the task of an educator willingly, because I love the task and am not lacking the ability to do it. Therefore, I stood in a completely honest relationship to him: I understood at once, of course, that from a lad of sixteen, whose eyes flickered at the sight of any flower girl, of whom there are so many in the Citta del Fiori, and all of whom—to speak *par parenthèse*—are very good-natured,[3] that there was no point in desiring or demanding from such a young man not only that he learn his lessons, but in general, it was useless to expect any work from him outside the classroom. When would he have had the time? He had to parade himself in a splendid carriage in the *piazetta* every day,[4] appear in various loges in the theater, and so on. On the other hand, I also understood very well that, with a young man who, once he reads an interesting page, retains it forever in his memory, or returning home from hearing a new opera, he sits down to play all its outstanding passages with harmonic chords and orchestral effects—you could do so much in four hours a day, and I conscientiously left him all the free time he wanted and could use. The main thing was that I understood the uselessness and even the positive harmfulness of various prohibitive measures, and I laughed heartily, sometimes insanely, when he showed me the lines crossed out in his history of the Roman emperors by his extremely moral tutor. Alas! It was precisely these lines that he had learned by heart, of course, from another copy of the same book. But the greatest miracle of the prohibitory system was revealed when the wise and respectable tutor, on his birthday

3. "City of Flowers" [Florence] (It.); "in parentheses" (It.).

4. "Small square" (It.).

(his pupil was already sixteen and was well acquainted with the better half of a certain very old and stingy Greek, who nevertheless followed the general rule of educated society and had his own loge in the Pergola) and presented him with a copy of *The Family Shakespeare*.[5] Although the Englishman knew Shakespeare very badly, and, it seems, in his soul considered him to be an indecent and immoral writer, he still saw with a grief-stricken heart, the vital necessity of deciding on such a gift. . . . That's where one could learn definitively the purpose of publishing *The Family Shakespeare* and other *editiones castratae* for the benefit of young people.[6] The first thing the youth did, it goes without saying, was to pilfer my copy of the non-family Shakespeare, and scrupulously insert all the omitted or bowdlerized passages into his copy, carefully learn them by heart, and shamelessly torture his virtuous supervisor with them every morning. . . .

And of course, *The Family Shakespeare* and, in general, other prohibitory measures, when applied to lively and talented natures, can't lead to any other results. . . . On the other hand, of course, one should not put everything into the hands of youth. Therefore, it turns out that my father was completely right in casting a blind eye on everything, so that his paternal dignity wouldn't suffer, nor would the freedom of human development be constrained in any way.

At the end of the 1820s and beginning of the 1830s, of course, neither M. Voltaire's *Candide*, nor *Les Voyages d'Antenor*, nor *Friend Matvey*, nor even *Faublas*, was in circulation among the usual readers of *Odds and Ends*.[7] I got to know all these splendid and instructive works afterward, at a later time, after my student years had ended. The current of arrogantly rational or cynically sensual contemplation of life, running through these prerevo-

5. The Pergola refers to a famous theater in Florence. *The Family Shakespeare* was an expurgated edition of Shakespeare's plays published in 1807.

6. "Castrated [or bowdlerized] editions" (Lat.).

7. The first Russian satirical magazine published in the second half of the eighteenth century, during the reign of Catherine II.

lutionary products,[8] had already dissipated and was replaced by another one, which had already run off in turn—so to speak, a reactionary current. The Middle Ages, as a period of darkness and ignorance, which had been rejected by the "Age of Reason," took their revenge. They occupied man's imagination almost entirely, though at first it was through the novelty of revival, and completely misunderstood at that. Chivalry, on the one hand, the mysteries of a world beyond the grave and strong passions with dark misdeeds on the other—this is what provoked the public taste for some time, which had tired of both the arrogance of naked reason and the unceremonious sensuality of former times. Even *Faublas* itself stands, so to speak, on the boundary of two movements: a tale, the intrigue of which is very confused and complex, plays a role in it which is no less sensual—and the story of Lodoi, which contains the entire character of the following era, the novels of Madame de Genlis and Madame Cottin. The tale, intrigue, the magical and mysterious, had to occupy human minds for some time—namely, because the extreme limits of revolutionary thought and reflection were the extreme limits of its own exhaustion. After the fanatically sensual cult of reason of the Hébertists, and the sentimentally dry cult of a higher being, acknowledged and sanctified by Robespierre, there was nowhere else to go.[9] It's remarkable that the very sanctifying of that cult by the virtuous Jean-Jacques Rousseau was already merging with the absurd ravings and mysteries of the widow Catherine Théot.[10] Moreover, satiated with the vanity of various future utopias, all of which failed one

8. Referring to the French Revolution of 1789–1793.

9. Jacques René Hébert (1757–1794) was a French journalist and the founder and editor of the extreme radical newspaper *Le Père Duchesne* during the French Revolution. Maximilien Robespierre (1758–1794) was a leader of the French Revolution best known for spearheading the Reign of Terror. He was an important member of the Jacobin political party.

10. Catherine Théot (1716–1794) was a French visionary. She gained notoriety when she was accused of being involved in a plot to overthrow the Republic; the downfall of Robespierre was attributed in part to her prophecies.

after another, humanity turned back for a while and transferred its dreams to the past.

Of course, this development occurred primarily in the country where the revolutionary movement was achieved in real life, not merely in thought, that is, in France, and if one turns to the tales that provoked and pleased the taste of the first postrevolutionary generation, one must absolutely keep in mind and strictly distinguish the currents that ran through the novels, for example, of the Englishwoman Ann Radcliffe, and the conscientious governess of the Duke of Orleans, Madame de Genlis, or the tearful Madame Cottin and the virtuously sentimental Ducray-Dumenil—as well as the Germans Clauren and Spiess.[11] All of this may have a common point of departure, which can possibly be called the restoration of the Middle Ages, but the word "restoration" may not be synonymous everywhere with the word "reaction."

Ann Radcliffe's talent, for example, and her magic effect on experienced readers—leave no doubt whatsoever. The late A. V. Druzhinin in one of his *Letters of a Country Subscriber*, with his usual qualities of keenness and sensitivity, wrote several brilliant, and even aesthetically profound, pages about the significance and enthralling power of many parts in the works of this now forgotten romantic writer, sincerely communicating his impressions of this painting of gloomy vaults and cellars, primitive passions and, at the same time, the purest English moral views of life—a painting, whose color palette is absolutely similar to Rembrandt's . . . but he didn't touch on the historical causes, which lay at the basis of this art and which brought it into being, and didn't delve into the immeasurable difference that lay between that genre and the already completely pure reactionary restoration, which was subsequently perfected by Walter Scott in his novels.[12] The point,

11. Carl Gottlieb Samuel Heun (1771–1854), better known by his pen name Heinrich Clauren, was a German author of many ghost stories. Christian Heinrich Spiess (1755–1799) was a German writer of romances and later pulp fiction, and horror stories.

12. See chapter VIII.

it seems to me, is that the attitudes of the famous woman romantic to the world she depicted were not as well-defined, of course, as Scott's attitudes to his world, because first of all she was lacking in his enormous store of information; but her attitudes were hardly less direct; her taste and reflection were hardly less organically formed. . . . To some extent Walter Scott *fashioned himself*, while Ann Radcliffe *was born*, born directly with her passion for ruins, cellars, and graves, with her nervous receptivity to the life of shades, visions, and ghosts, and with her sensitivity to gloomy and primitive passions—and she was born from the very depths of the English spirit, from that same gloomy spleen, which expressed itself in that nation's greatest representative in Hamlet's graveyard scene, and was later concentrated in Byron with powerful, one-sided concentration. I'm speaking here, of course, not about the degree of talent, but about its sources; I'm speaking about the fact that Ann Radcliffe was a profoundly genuine talent—which explains her distinguished, leading, and magical effect on the thoughts of her readers, the colossal success of her novels everywhere, shaken, but not too quickly, only by the success of the extremely skillful constructs of the Scottish novelist.

On the other hand, writers of chivalric novels in Germany, for example, Spiess, Clauren (it seems that he is the author of *The Gravedigger*, *Urns in a Lonely Valley*, and others)—though constantly concerned with chivalry, the fantastic, and the Middle Ages, didn't belong to the subsequent reactionary restoration of that period, the consequences of which were: the contrived, artificial Catholicism of Görres and the Schlegel Brothers, and the "impudent" madness of the "doctor of love," Zacharias Werner, "that madman who imagined himself to be a poet," as he was brilliantly called by the witty author of *Letters on Dilettantism in Science.*[13] Spiess and, in general, the writers of the German chivalric novels of that

13. Heinrich Clauren (1771–1854) became one of the most popular German authors of fiction for the middle class in the first half of the nineteenth century. But these novels were in fact written by Baron Ludwig von Bilderbek. Johann Görres (1776–1848) was a German writer, philosopher, theologian, historian, and journalist;

time belonged to a different period, and the so-called Sturm und Drang of German literature, a period begun by the Bacchanalian outpourings of Klopstock and his friends before the *Irmin Säule*, and expressing itself in the most brilliant manner in Goethe's iron-fisted *Götz von Berlichingen* and Schiller's *Die Räuber*—a period that was destructive, rather than reactionary.[14] Ancient Germany, then chivalry and the Middle Ages were banners of battle for this titanic generation, but not of rest, and the dagger without a signature burned over the unmarked grave of the foolish murderer of the philistine Kotzebue,[15] was a direct consequence of the Teutonic revolutionary movement. Naturally, all this is related not to Spiess's long and boring novels, but to the tendency in whose wake these and similar novels limped, to that current that runs in them.

I know—I can't help making another digression—today's younger generation, if it only skims my notes (which is very doubtful), will reproach me for obscurity and even my vagueness of exposition—but then, after all, I can't really write entire volumes to explain things that are close to me and my contemporaries and that are well known, although, of course, on the other hand, I can't demand that the younger generation read all that nonsense like *Knights of the Lion*, *Knights of Semigor*, *Ullo*, *Old Man in the Mountain*, and *An Old Man Everywhere and Nowhere*—that we read.[16] In any case, I can reasonably demand

---

the Schlegel Brothers (August and Friedrich) were German poets, translators, and critics, and leading influences within Jena Romanticism. Zacharias Werner (1768–1823) was a German poet of mystical-Masonic inclination, a dramatist, and a preacher. Actually the quotation belongs to Alexander Herzen, but the censor prevented Grigoryev from mentioning his name.

14. An "Irminsul" was a sacred, pillar-like object attested as playing an important role in the Germanic paganism of the Saxons. *Götz von Berlichingen* is a successful 1773 drama by Goethe, based on the memoirs of the historical adventurer-poet Götz von Berlichingen (ca. 1480–1562). *The Robbers* is the first drama by the German poet and playwright Friedrich Schiller. It was published in 1781.

15. August von Kotzebue (1761–1819) was a German dramatist and writer who also worked as a consul in Russia. He was murdered in 1819 by Karl Sand, a member of a radical student organization.

16. A list of Russian translations of Western chivalric novels.

a general knowledge of the course of literary history and the meaning of literary periods from whoever pleases to cut the pages of the *Epoch* with the intention of skimming them, and I can conscientiously inform him of the necessity of possessing that general knowledge. I have no time to relate the history of German, English, or French literature, since I am devoting myself to those tendencies, which they conveyed to our generation, so I must necessarily limit myself to allusions.

The current, which runs through these old chivalric German novels, is very complex. Those persecuted virtuous men and the innocent people oppressed by villains, who are always protected either outright by mysterious forces from beyond the grave, or else by virtuous knights, obliged by the rules of their order to combat evil and to support the suffering truth; these secret tribunals, Femgerichte,[17] dealing out justice and truth with a hidden dagger, in an unjust society lacking unity (which Germany has yet to achieve even today), this gloom and mystery that surround the champions of justice, some sort of Knights of the Lion or Semigor, that eternal chalice of the Holy Grail, soaring in the heights of the heavens—all that is not simply love for the Middle Ages or desire for the restoration—far from it. It included eighteenth-century mesmerism with its spirits and spiritualists, as well as the Illuminism of Weishaupt or Rosicrucianism with their mysteries,[18] symbols, and hidden daggers—it contained, finally and primarily, the terrible conviction of the complete lawlessness of a disunited society and the no less terrible conviction of the absolute necessity for that constant action of supernatural, super-social, and therefore antisocial forces—a conviction expressed by Germany's two great authors in *Karl*

17. Originally, the local Westphalian courts of the Middle Ages, which developed into a secret organization in Germany.

18. Johann Adam Weishaupt (1748–1830) was a German philosopher, professor of civil law and later canon law, and founder of the Illuminati, a society similar to the Masons; Rosicrucianism is a spiritual movement that arose in Europe in the early seventeenth century, also similar to the Masons.

Moor and *Götz von Berlichingen* and in life by Sand's mad martyrdom. There is nothing astonishing that no matter how bad or long the inventions of Spiess, Clauren, and other chivalric novelists of that time were, the currents running through them made a powerful impact on the imagination and emotions of the reading masses.

And finally, as far as French novels of this period are concerned, they were also distinguished by a special character, not one of reaction, or even restoration. I'm speaking, of course, about novels that became widespread among the public, that is, the reading crowd, the novels of Ducray-Duminil, Mmes. Genlis and Cottin, and the novels of Chateaubriand and Mme. De Stahl. *Victor, or A Child of the Woods*, *The Blind Man at St. Catherine's Spring*—all works by the first novelist mentioned, *The Knights of the Swan* by Mme. Genlis—and the famous *Mathilde or The Crusade* by Mme. Cottin—these novels are what provided the reading public's daily fare, especially its "female half." Ducray-Duminil appealed by his complicated and entangled intrigues and his various horrors, which were very carefully thought out, even if they weren't subtle. An incalculable amount of tears was shed over *Mathilde,* and young ladies were positively enamored with Malek-Adel, precisely until that time when he was replaced by the heroes of the Vicomte de Arlencourt's heroes, the representatives of a new, now purely restoration and counterrevolutionary stream. The most boring of all were the novels of Mme. Genlis, although by a strange twist of fate in her vulgar invention, *The Knights of the Swan*, previously mentioned, the French prerevolutionary spirit and its attitude at that time to the Middle Ages, chivalry, and so forth, so that even the many extremely scandalous indecencies in the works of the cold and proper Governess of Orleans, and the instability of her general view of life demonstrates that her acquaintance with the works of Voltaire, and with Voltaire himself, did not pass without a trace. And the knights, too, borrowed by her without the least familiarity with the history of the time of Charlemagne, do not resemble at all those in German novels: these are very light-headed and frivolous people—and without her knowing it, of course, they emerged in her works as typically French, and even Provençal knights—or *raisonneurs*, rational men, resembling the French bourgeoisie just like two drops of water. I won't expound on Mme. Cottin, because even though she may have been more widely read, she was in essence less typical. Ducray-Duminil, as I said above, attracted readers by the intricacy of his plots. But what is extremely important in all these novelists, who differed so much from one another, is that in all of them—if we are also to add Mme. Montelieu, the author of *Caroline de Lichtfield* and *Amalia, or a Hut in the Mountains*,[19] were famous at that time—despite all their vulgarity, the general French spirit and the end of the eighteenth century are expressed very clearly and plainly and in a lighthearted, sensitive, bourgeois rationality of their view of life. That morality to which they incline, and the moral that is deduced from them, differs completely from Radcliffe's affected Puritanism or the virtue preached by Spiess. It's naked and dry to the highest degree of vulgarity, neither wrapped in splenetic gloom, nor encircled by a halo of mystery, and it's completely practical. These contrivances were written through purely external impulses, not at all through inner ones. It was not the striving for the Middle Ages, for the mysterious or the horrible that gave birth to them with their crusades, castles, dungeons, mysteries, and horrors, but simple fashion and fancy. The taste for robbers came from Schiller, that is, from M. Gilles, *auteur allemande*,[20] to whom the young republic sent a patent of citizenship and whose Karl Moor transformed himself on the French stage into Robert, *chef des brigands*;[21] mystery, dungeons,

19. Grigoryev is in error: the latter novel was written by Nikolai Zryakhov, the author of several quasi-historical novels published in the 1840s. Isabelle de Montolieu wrote a novel titled *The Hut in the High Alps* (1813), translated into Russian in 1817.

20. "German author" (Fr.).

21. "Chief of the brigands" (Fr.).

and horrors were simply competition to the enormous success of Ann Radcliffe's novels. Nothing like this had ever attracted the French seriously before. Madame de Staël's notable book, *De l'Allemagne* had not yet appeared, and Chateaubriand was carefully planning his *Genie du christianisme*, and still carried the psychological confessions of René and Eudora only in his heart.[22] There were simply written tales, that tried to interest the reader by larding through sentimentalism, on the one hand, with which sensuality was covered, like a fig leaf and, on the other hand, morality, which in translation to pure French meant then, and always means, as is well known, rationality. But it is precisely in that hypocrisy that these vulgar artifices destined for use by the reading public, are important. The hypocrisy of sentimentalism and morality are completely comprehensible after the sensual saturnalia begun by the philosopher Diderot and concluded by the Marquis de Sade.

There was, however, another current, even more delayed, but on the other hand, far more genuinely murky, in which the old, prerevolutionary eighteenth century manifested itself in absolutely bestial eructations. This stream ran powerfully in the works of one of the writers who was also one of the favorites of the reading public, Pigault-Lebrun.[23] He was simply a cynical writer, although one must pay him his due: he was incomparably more talented than all the sentimentalists, and incomparably less repulsive than the favorite of the following period, Paul de Kock,[24] with an indisputable comic force, blatant honesty about depravity, without the slightest pretense to morality and

22. *On Germany* (Fr.: *De l'Allemagne*), is a book about German culture and, in particular, German Romanticism, written by the French writer Germaine de Staël (1766–1817). François-René, vicomte de Chateaubriand (1768–1848) was a French writer, politician, diplomat and historian who had a notable influence on the literature of the nineteenth century.

23. Pigault-Lebrun (1753–1835) was a popular French novelist, playwright, and Epicurean.

24. Paul de Kock (1793–1871) was a French low-brow novelist. who acquired a literary reputation for low-brow output in poor taste.

virtue, which in Paul de Kock are far more offensive to healthy aesthetic and moral feelings than his salaciousness. The works of that extremely candid gentleman, I think, can't be read today without laughter; he knew how to draw even the characters and figures, and whoever has read his novel *The Page* has not forgotten the very gallant Hussar Brandt, the Baron Felzheim's true friend and his young son's faithful tutor, the pleasant scenes at the station with the lady, with the old cynic, and the red-headed Capuchin. . . . The directness and candor of the Voltairianism, with his contempt for *monacaille*,[25] and Diderotism, with his fanatical worship for sensuality, are heard most naively in scenes like these. I can't consign Pigault-Lebrun even to the ranks of *harmful* writers; he demonstrates depravity so unceremoniously, so denuded of any attractive and provocative adornments, that it could hardly tempt anyone. I recall that when my father, for example, read *The Page* aloud, he would send me to my room for a short time, and later, as I have already recounted, I stole the book in my usual way and, of course, I read with a certain feverish agitation the sections that he'd omitted: they had no particular effect on me, as far as I can remember; I laughed exceedingly, because it was really very humorous; the man wrote in a much more amusing way than Paul de Kock (whose works, moreover, I could never tolerate).

But the whole point is that Pigault-Lebrun, a bold and forthright man, who arrogantly presented himself as an immoral writer, demanding pro forma that the youthful imagination be distanced from acquaintance with such a cynic. And it was exactly only pro forma because it would never occur to anyone to drive me out of the room when they were reading "Nature and Love," "Walter, a Child of the Battlefield," and other works by the most immoral authors of the time, equally compounded of the most venomous and tempting sensuality and of virtue of the most maudlin German style, and even of the German, August

25. Monasticism (Fr.).

von Lafontaine, known for his morality and virtue.[26] To many people, especially those who recall a line from Pushkin:

> A novel in Lafontaine's style.[27]

My judgment about the immorality of that novelist and others like him will most likely seem paradoxical; but in reality, if one is going to talk about immorality or the harm done by works of literature, then it will turn out exactly like this. The young heart and even, to put it simply, young sensuality, does not submit as easily as is generally thought, to the cynical impudence, doesn't conceal itself under the cover of debauchery. One has to work up to that step, and at first there must absolutely be attractions, adornments, and a certain mystery, something that conveys a certain charm to this forbidden fruit. A disciplined person is at first attracted by such qualities in a woman herself. . . .

Among readers even of the not so young generation, but only somewhat younger than the one I belong to, no one, of course, has read the sentimental-sensual nonsense of the virtuous German novelist—for which I congratulate them with all my heart, because the time that would have been wasted on that completely vacuous and frivolous reading, could probably have been spent more profitably on games played outdoors, and the anxious feelings that would certainly have been aroused in their beings, would have found later, appropriately, a correct and real outlet, and not one in books. On the other hand, I'm not at all ashamed to admit that I read these books and they had a great influence on my own development. That's how it really was: how was I to blame?

---

26. Works by Jean de La Fontaine (1621–1695), a French fabulist and one of the most widely read French poets of the seventeenth century. August von Lafontaine (1758–1831) was the enormously popular German author of sentimental and didactic tales of domestic life.

27. From Pushkin's *Eugene Onegin* (1825), chapter 4, stanza 50.

Just try to imagine, for example, this ridiculous incident: there lives in some remote German town a dance master who was virtuous and honest to a pathetic and maudlin degree. He is joined in marriage, of course, to an equally virtuous and beautiful maiden, even poorer than he is; they live together properly, that is, like a pair of canaries, endlessly showering each other with kisses and feeding each other their modest meals. Nevertheless, they produce a son, Walter. He turns out to be the model of purity and virtue. In his early youth he meets some wandering maiden, also the image of purity, virtue, and innocence; he befriends her and passes time with her in the purest manner, preserving, although not without anxiety, and very alarming anxiety, her chastity. How he manages to do this, you should ask the virtuous writer, who places him as though on purpose in the most difficult situations. . . . Then, by precisely what fates I can't really say, because the thread of this story has disappeared from my memory, and if I were to decide to reread it, you would be absolutely right to suspect me of gross stupidity—Walter ends up in some sort of wealthy house of a strange old eccentric, who has a lovely and totally innocent niece, age sixteen. For some reason the old man has to hide his niece from someone for a month and, at the same time, be convinced of Walter's virtue. There is a remote little house in his enormous garden, a cage for the pair of canaries—and in that little house, completely alone, he settles Walter and Leopoldina, obliging Walter, on his word of honor, to respect the chastity of the beautiful girl entrusted to him; he doesn't say a word to her, of course, because he assumed that "young girls are hard of hearing," always and everywhere. You can imagine what a hellishly exasperating life these poor doves lead for that whole month. I suppose that Kukushkina, who would faint in ecstasy when she reads "how obstacles vanished and the two hearts that loved each other were united," would reread this idyll not once or twice, but some twenty times. The story is called "Walter, a Child of the Battlefield," in the Russian translation, of course.

By the way, it's not Walter who's the child of the battlefield, but a young child who's really found during the course of a battle and is raised by him. I have forgotten, I repeat, what the plot is.

Here's another story that always particularly enchanted my father, at a time when he was living mostly on his memories, but liked to tease himself, delighting, like Kukushkina—the story is called "Nature and Love." You know, of course, that the last quarter of the eighteenth century went crazy over nature, in its pristine purity and innocence, and tried to re-create it artificially—as Wagner created the Homunculus in the second part of Goethe's *Faust*—finally to create somehow man from nature. The great eloquent sophist, the most conscientious and zealous of them, because first of all he'd deceived himself, Rousseau, placed in circulation both the theory of the absolute rights of passions in his novel *Julie*, and the theory, removed from the conditions of education in his *Emile*, and he created a general utopia in his *Contrat social*—if he didn't conceive of "nature at the end of the eighteenth century" (because before him there was no lack of creators of it), then at least by the force of his fiery talent and captivating eloquence, and his life itself, full of torments because of his absurd ideas and prosecution for that idea, he launched it full sail.[28] (Persecuted by everyone—both the Catholics, and the Calvinists, and even by the philosophes themselves, showered with abuse and slander by Desfontaines and other similar characters,[29] but together with Voltaire's merciless sarcasm, he nonetheless triumphed for a period of time after his death. Not only do all kinds of travelers go to pay homage at his tomb (remember how some Englishman, without any previous conversation, asked Karamzin directly, who was deep

28. Jean Jacques Rousseau's (1712–1778) major works included: *Julie, ou la nouvelle Heloise* (1761), *Emile* (1761), and *The Social Contract* (1762).

29. Grigoryev is confusing Abbé Pierre Guyot-Desfontaines (1685–1745), a French journalist, translator, and popular historian, with Madame du Deffand (1697–1780), woman of letters and a leading figure in French society, who really did shower abuse on Rousseau.

in thought: "Vous pensez à lui?), his words pass into deeds, the bloody acts of his practical students, Saint-Just and Robespierre, while on the other hand, are spread as doctrine among the reading masses.[30] As a deed, it dies out in its turn, but it dies in a grandiose and strict way; as the booty of the reading masses, it is vulgarized completely in such sentimental romances as:

> For love alone has nature
> Brought us into the world,

to Gessner's saccharine idylls and his tale of the first seafarer, to the novel *Nature and Love* by August Lafontaine.[31]

Some eccentric brings up his son *à la Emile*, but with even greater extremes, in absolute isolation from human intercourse, in complete ignorance of its conditions and attitudes, even the differences between the sexes—most likely so that if he finds everything out for himself, it will seem sweeter to him. . . . But there emerges from this not a canvas for *Huron, ou l'ingénu*—that aptly venomous yet profound mockery of fashionable "nature" by old man Voltaire, in spite of its carefree tone—but a completely different story.[32] Young William—of course as appropriate—is the model of purity, integrity, and innocence. At his first contact with society, he comes across a certain maiden, Fanny, and, immediately despairing over her complete lack of comprehension of "nature," and her very shrewd understanding of feminine coquetry and faithlessness—he goes off to faraway India. There, of course, he learns to respect deeply the wild

---

30. "Are you thinking about him [Rousseau]?" (Fr.). Louis de Saint-Just (1767–94) was a French revolutionary, political philosopher, member and president of the French National Convention.

31. Salomon Gessner was a Swiss painter, newspaper publisher, and poet, best known for his idylls.

32. *Huron, ou l'ingénue* is a satirical novella (1767) that tells the story of a man from the Huron tribe who is transported to Paris in 1690. In it, Voltaire satirizes religious doctrine, government corruption, and the injustices of French society.

natives and to hate the civilization that oppresses them, the "children of nature," civilization, and there he meets the lovely Nagida. Even her name—of course changed in such a way by the Russian translator, who apparently fulfilled his task "with gusto," demonstrates that this is bare, pure nature. And in reality, various scenes under palm trees and banana trees completely convince the reader of this, and his nerves are seriously agitated whether he is a youth, who still knows nothing, or an old man, who knows a great deal and is reliving his experiences in his mind. No wonder my father enjoyed reading that work so much—and not because he was convinced of the superiority of the primitive ways over those of civilization. . . .

All these, as you can see, were more or less murky streams, belated currents, but they brought their silt and slime into our development.

VIII

Walter Scott and New Currents

Meanwhile new currents were already intruding into the intellectual and moral life, even into the life lagging behind the general development, in which I was being brought up. Naturally, I'm speaking about the backwardness of the conditions in relation to the older generation, born in the last half of the eighteenth century. The younger generation lived primarily according to the intellectual and moral tendencies of contemporary life, which I had put apparently first and foremost in complete fairness, although, it was organically connected to the generation that had given birth to it, and couldn't avoid receiving a certain part of its heritage of its impressions. On the other hand, the older generation, if only it wasn't too decrepit, and was still in contact with real life, and consequently with the generation that was just entering the arena of life, also couldn't avoid, to some degree, a share of the new impressions of the younger generation.

Not only my father, a man, who although he'd received a superficial, but to some extent, a full and encyclopedic education for his epoch—even his friends from the service who were really very poorly educated, and who could take an interest in nothing but bribes, inventories, and wine cellars—even they had not only heard of Pushkin, but had even read some of his works. The small fraction of their time that was free from work and wine cellars they sometimes used for reading, well, perhaps, due to getting overly drunk—and, even with a very small, though still significant, share of the money left after paying their living expenses, they would purchase books, although in a state of drunkenness, acquiring them, of course, primarily at the Smolensk market or at the Sukharyev tower; some of them even tried to create a sort of library. A mania for such completely useless purchases, in their wives' opinion, spread when Russian historical novels started to pour forth in an uncontrollable stream. Here even the drunkest secretary at the City Magistrate's office, who was never in a sober state, read a book and even bought it from the dealer, although I can't say precisely whether he bought it when he was drunk because he'd read it before, or read it because he'd bought it when he was drunk. That was *Tanka the Robber*,[1] who seemed particularly enchanting because the heroine had a knout in her hands—so it seems he bought a little box to hold tobacco because it had such a picture of this new illustrious woman on the cover.

But Russian historical novels already belong to the following stream, not to this one, which ended at the beginning of the 1830s, and included only the first novels by Zagoskin and Bulgarin,[2] the first experiments of Russian genius in that genre.

As is well known, the Russian genius discovered this genre not on its own, but took it over and demonstrated its independence in astonishing simplification and as its exceptional consequences of this simplification, its enormous fertility—about which I will speak in greater detail, of course, at the appropriate time and place.

---

1. A popular nineteenth-century historical tale (1834) by Sergei Rostokinsky.
2. A reference to Zagoskin's *Yury Miloslavsky* (1829) and Bulgarin's *Dmitry the Pretender* (1830).

In that sliver of time, about which in the meantime I'm still speaking—the novels of the famous Scottish novelist, or, as it was popular to refer to him in the high style in almanacs and even some journal articles, the "Scottish bard"—were the new currents for the obsolete generation and for the reading public in general.

The "Scottish bard," who at one time aroused enthusiasm bordering on adulation to the point of worship, swallowed, devoured, and read unceasingly by all of Europe in decent translations, and by us in absolutely abominable Russian versions—giving birth both to epistles from poets, as, for example, from our Kozlov, and whole books about him—like the tome by some incredibly limited Scotsman, called Olin Cunningham,[3] full of indecent, stupid adoration, which knows no bounds—the Scottish bard, I say, among us had already retreated into the past—and no longer arouses in us the previous enthusiasm—nevertheless he could still arouse fanaticism. It is a fact, and an indubitable one—whether it's sad or happy I leave that decision ad libitum—that at the end of the 1820s and during the 1830s, although published in dull, gray form, translated execrably and, from Defauconpret's French translations,[4] his novels went through many editions and were purchased in spite of the fact that they were not inexpensive; they were sold in large quantities, while in the mid-1840s, in Petersburg a cheap and rather decent translation of the original works by Walter Scott was issued, but, as far as I know, it ceased after only four novels—and those were bought in very small numbers. In the 1850s, some kind man in Moscow began to publish an even cheaper edition, translated from the original, though even grayer than the Petersburg version, and issued a rather tolerable version of *The Legend of Montrose*—he stopped at that, probably because

3. See Ivan Kozlov's "To Walter Scott" (1832). A translation of Allan Cunningham, *Some Account of the Life and Works of Sir Walter Scott* (published in 1835).

4. Auguste Defauconpret (1767–1843) was a French translator and writer; his translations were published in Paris from 1822 to 1830.

there were few buyers—while a very large number of the old translation, under the title of *The Meritorious Officer*, or *Montrose's War*, had been sold.

Habent sua fata libelli is a very old proverb,[5] bruised and worn to vulgarity, but still extremely true, only applied mainly to temporary, so to speak, fashionable (not, by the way, in a vulgar way, but in a significant, Hegelian sense of the word), and not to the eternal manifestations of art.

First of all, I must say that I count the renowned Scottish novelist among such fashionable manifestations in art, though in its own way, an absolutely extraordinary manifestation. To repeat this statement in our day after the greatest of English thinkers, Thomas Carlyle,[6] is, of course, not at all audacious, but the fact is that even in my early youth I read many of Walter Scott's famous novels without being thunderstruck, and, on the contrary, read them several times over, and from my childhood until my youth, with constantly lively interest, even some of his less famous works as well. *Ivanhoe*, for example, made a very small impression on me, and I don't hesitate to say that as far as narrative interest is concerned, that celebrated novel comes far below the stories of Dumas, and only such details and characters, which are not valuable to the author, because it's obvious that the reader is far more partial to the passionate, but dishonorable Brian the Templar than to the virtuously stupid knight Ivanhoe. . . . Absolutely no impression was made on me by *Waverly* and *Woodstock*, whose Oliver Cromwell is so wooden and pale in comparison with the living figure presented in all his glory in Victor Hugo's great play,[7] and *Quentin Durward*, whose much acclaimed Louis XI of the greatest poet of our century, though in his *Notre Dame* he used him in only two scenes. But then, what fine scenes they are, full of such power and poetry!

5. "Books have their own destiny" (Lat.).

6. Thomas Carlyle (1795–1881) was a Scottish essayist, historian, and philosopher, who wrote a lengthy article about Walter Scott's life and works in 1847.

7. *Cromwell* (1827).

Nor did *Richard in Palestine* produce much of an impression on me, and the same for *Carl the Brave* and *Anne of Geierstein*, the sentimental *Edinburgh Prison*, and *Kenilworth*, the last of which is completely built on special effects. I'm not even ashamed to admit that I like *The Bride of Lammermoor* as much as the opera *Lucia*, that is, as the inspiration of Maestro Donizetti and the singer Rubini, and not as Scott's novel, and it seems to me ("Oh! barbarism!" the belated worshippers of the Scottish bard will shout) that the commonplace librettist Felici Romani squeezed out of the novel all the juice of the real drama contained in the novel, diluting its dramatic essence with the tap water of unavoidable Italian vulgarities.

In the meantime, I read and reread in various translations and, at last, read the original of *The Pirate* or *The Sea Robber*, as it is called in the fresh and elegant translation, though it was made from the French, by the Zamoskvorechye novelist, Mr. Voskresensky. I read and reread *Montrose*, and read and reread *Peveril of the Peak*. Yes! Even up to now that entire world with its circumstances, all its foggy gray color, solitary, enclosed, as it were, isolated from the rest of the world, is still alive before me, the little world of the Scottish islands, where the simple, not even historical action takes place, unfettered by any brilliant personalities and events, but full of drama of its own life, which takes place in the novel *The Pirate*, or, as it is called in Mr. Voskresensky's version, *The Sea Robber*.

The Legend of Montrose, known also as *The Meritorious Officer* or *Montrose's War*, as it was called in its old gray-covered Russian translation, made an equally enormous impression on me. I won't even mention *Peveril*. I didn't read it in my childhood and came upon it in the original only later, but, in any case, I consider it among the stronger impressions produced by Walter Scott. Then there's something strange: I read one of his narrative poems several times in a useless translation titled "Marmion, or the Battle at Flodenfield." Zhukovsky made a splendid translation of a famous excerpt from it, "The Tale of the Crypt," but I repeat, I didn't make the acquaintance of his well-rendered excerpt until much later.

In our house, Walter Scott was not particularly popular, and was read with comparatively less enthusiasm than other writers. As far as I recall, my father didn't even read *The Pirate* to the end—he found it so boring. Although he did finish *The Meritorious Officer*, he complained about its long-windedness. The family barely tolerated ten pages of *Marmion*. In general, the form of exposition—genuinely new, and moreover dramatic in the works of the Scottish novelist—somehow alienated the older generation of readers. "When he starts carrying on those endless conversations of his," my father used to say, "it's simply deadly, to tell the truth," and he would skip over a few pages without a twinge of conscience. The depiction of character toward which Walter Scott always aspired didn't interest him in the least. Like many of his contemporaries, what they liked most in a novel was an interesting plot, and therefore, the works of the renowned novelist appealed to him only when he was writing about important historical personalities, or, as in *Count Robert of Paris*, he was relating curious adventures.

Reflecting subsequently on the reasons for my lack of sympathy for many of Walter Scott's most admired works, and, on the other hand, for my strong sympathy for the novels mentioned above, I found that I was completely correct through some inner sense.

Art remains long-lasting and acts profoundly on the soul primarily through one trait (besides the artist's talent, of course)—the sincerity of his motives or impulses, on which the faith of the artist in the world created by him depends, but as it says in the Scriptures, "without faith it's not possible to please God"; nor is it possible to satisfy people completely.

The Scotsman was a son of a mountainous land to his fingertips, who strictly maintained its traditions, a member of a clan, although it became part of the general structure of the English nation, and voluntarily at that, not like the Irish nation, nevertheless preserving its identity and a certain reserve—Walter Scott was completely filled with a superstitious love for the archaic, the legends, and the exiled or oppressed peoples, for overthrown dynasties, those remnants of an ancient, self-contained way of life that in some places still remained intact.

Whether accidentally or not, his activity coincided with aspirations for restoration, which were manifested after the first revolution throughout Europe. But—once again—these aspirations differed in various European countries. In Germany—as I've already said—a revolutionary vein was pulsating under these aspirations for restoration; in France they were a reaction temporarily needed, but reborn in the new revolution of 1830; in our country, finally, they were and remained simple strivings toward the purification of our national integrity, our native and historical identity, oppressed for a while by the terrorism of the reform, or cowed and obscured, also temporarily, by the veneer of Western civilization.

This is still not the place to speak about us and our tendencies toward restoration. I have already spoken in sufficient detail about Germany. To clarify my idea about the immediate, unreflective aspiration to restoration in Walter Scott's literary activity, I must say a few words about the French tendencies toward restoration.

But by no means about those that were expressed in the brilliant literary activity of one of France's greatest writers, Chateaubriand—that hero René, profoundly shaken by events and terribly shattered in his inner world—who held onto the old Catholic and feudal order with absolute sincerity and with the most ardent enthusiasm, as though to a rescuing anchor.[8] He always appears to me as some sort of Saint Dominic, passionately, with all the ardor of a shaken soul and broken heart, with all

8. René was the hero of Chateaubriand's short novella, which first appeared in 1802. The work had an immense impact on early Romanticism throughout Europe.

the convulsiveness of passion embracing the foot of the cross in one of Fra Beato's marvelous paintings in the monastery of San Marco in Florence. Nor will I accept as French restoration those aspirations, which were begun by Victor Hugo in his odes and were expressed in *Notre-Dame de Paris*, in *Le roi s'amuse*, and were brilliantly concluded with *Les Miserables*; nor the pompous meditations or harmonies of Lamartine.[9] As I already said, one must view an epoch in those manifestations where it is most clearly revealed.

At that time, the reading public was "raving" about the absolutely ordinary French novelist Vicomte d'Arlincourt, who is today completely forgotten and for good reason.[10] His *Mysterious Hermit* and his apostate *Agobar*, gloomy for effect, his *Foreign Lady*, marked by a curse, replaced the virtuous Malek-Adels and sentimental Mathildes in readers' minds. But they replaced them in quite a different manner than the author had intended. The author himself is the most limited of the writers of the restoration and reaction: in all of his many successful novels, he brings to the fore one principal feeling: love for the overturned and exiled dynasties—particularly in *The Renegade* and *Ipsiboé*, he makes us feel, so to speak, that the Merovingians of the first novel, or the Provençal of the second—are the same as Bourbons for him; but particularly not for the French reading public, but, for instance, let's say ours, who had nothing to do with the exploits of the maiden warrior Ezilda, full of love for an overturned dynasty, nor with Ipsiboé, wholeheartedly, though vainly, reestablishing the Bozons in Provence. For the French public, all that was already old stuff, but for ours, it was completely alien. The commonplace novelist didn't attract readers with that; rather it was his passionate French enthusiasm, which helped him turn into small change the powerful and monoto-

9. A reference to Lamartine's *Poetical Mediations* (1820) and its later sequels.

10. Charles-Victor Prévot, Vicomte d'Arlincourt (1788–1856), was a wildly popular French novelist who rivaled Victor Hugo in the 1820s.

nously gloomy images of the splenetic Englishman, to whom Lamartine wrote an enthusiastic epistle, and whom our Pushkin called, likening him to the sea, "the ruler of our thoughts,"[11] but before whom the reading masses bowed down by rumor and from far away, as to some mysteriously gloomy idol. *All These Hermits*, *Agobars*, and *Foreign Ladies* were unquestionably Byronism turned into small change; the change that may have been more accessible to the public than genuine Byronism. On the other hand, the well-known, feverish passion of the Frenchman, in some places penetrating the Vicomte d'Arlincourt's pieces, in some sense was already the harbinger of that great phase of literature called Young France. While the noble Vicomte's aspirations for restoration were expended by him completely in vain, and if he hadn't known, like a true Frenchman, how to serve both God and Mammon simultaneously, that is, if on the one hand, he didn't write so that even the reaction would not be repulsive and, at the same time, it would resemble the new passionate aspirations, he wouldn't have had absolutely any success.

The naive, immediate, sincerely restorational aspirations of Walter Scott were completely different—without even mentioning the enormous disparity in talent. Completely filled with the world of legends, which he himself collected with profound love of native songs and legends, foreign to all kinds of political problems and intentional tendencies, honest even to the point of extreme narrow-mindedness, which explains his ridiculous, but sincere history of the French Revolution and Napoleon, Walter Scott was the complete personification of the Scottish spirit, but without that terrible and grandiose side of it, which produced severe Puritanism and Oliver Cromwell, but from the everyday side of it, so to speak. One would have to search extensively to locate another bourgeois writer as narrow-minded as the "Scottish bard"—perhaps only our Zagoskin would be a suitable match: his virtuous characters are dumber than Yury Miloslavsky and

11. A reference to Pushkin's lyric "To the Sea" (1824).

Roslavlev, and more repulsive than Dickens's Charles brothers.[12] But the point is that he was still a poet, and a great poet, though far from being a genius like Byron or Hugo; he is a poet against his own will and desire because there arise before us in his works those same images, for which he feels no moral sympathy; and because on the other hand, there is both truth and poetic charm in the sympathy he feels for oppressed and fallen races, overturned, but once popular dynasties, for superstitions and legends—there is artistic fullness and beauty in his depictions of self-contained little worlds or types that have receded into the realm of the past.

What a world that is, for example, cut off completely from the rest of the world—this world of Scottish islands with its patriarch Magnus Troll (I'm taking all the names from Voskresensky's translation),[13] with his daughters: poetically gloomy, superstitious, nervous, and passionate Minna, with her fair-haired and simple sister, Brenda, with the mysterious, either insane or clairvoyant magician of the elements, Norna, with the enigmatic old adventurer Mertoun, with the brave brigand Cleveland, and his witty, indecently swearing comrade, with the eccentric bard Claud Halcro—and with the greedy, shrewd peddler, unceremoniously using shore rights. All that is alive, all that walks and talks right in front of us: it's as if we ourselves were at old Magnus's feast and were witnessing the old sword dance with our own eyes—as though we accompanied Magnus and his daughters through the dark night to have our fortune told by the mad witch; we stood with her with this fortuneteller on the cliff and invoked the sea wind; we even searched in the peddler's backpack and examined with curiosity the various miraculous items, collected by him unceremoniously as *res primi occupantis* in view of his shore rights;[14] finally, we believed,

12. From Charles Dickens's novel, *Nicholas Nickleby* (1838).

13. Scott's novel *The Pirate* (1821); the Russian translation was published in 1829.

14. *Res nullius naturaliter fit primi occupantis*—"the first person to occupy unowned property becomes its legal owner" (Lat.).

entering Norna's cave, that her dwarf was really some kind of gnome, and not a creature of this earthly world. And what did we care, following with feverish interest Minna's passion for the brave brigand and the magician's mysterious sympathy for him, for young Mertoun's vulgarities or for his sentimental attitude toward Brenda.

And the most lovable captain Dugald Dalgetty in *A Legend of Montrose*;[15] with enormous innocence and, in his own way, completely honest, ready to serve both the convent and the royalists, depending on who would pay him more—Dalgetty, captured by the republicans and prepared to go to the gallows because several days remained in his service to Montrose and the royalists—the learned captain Dalgetty, with his indecent (for the most part) Latin citations, with which he entertains the proper and gloomily mournful Puritan, Lady Argyle, at the table. . . . And the enmity of clans—and the community of the "children of the night," with their terrible superstitious, and at the same time, impious, gloomy, clairvoyant leader—and finally Allen MacAulay, clairvoyant as Saul, tormented by the furies and soothed only by the sounds of the beautiful Annot Lyle's harp. What do we care if she loves not him, but the vulgarian Earl of Menteith? A world, one that is real, and at the same time fantastic, is revealed to us; the characters, clearly sketched, live in our imagination—and the poet, apparently, is in his element. . . .

Such were the impressions of books, literary tendencies, surrounding my childhood. . . .

15. Scott's novel was published in 1819.

Selected Bibliography of Works in English on Grigoryev's Prose

Dowler, Wayne. *Dostoevsky, Grigor'ev, and Native Soil Conservatism*. Toronto: University of Toronto Press, 1982.

Dowler, Wayne. *An Unncessary Man: The Life of Apollon Grigor'ev*. Toronto: University of Toronto Press, 1995.

Matlaw, Ralph. "Apollon Grigoryev: An Introduction." *My Literary and Moral Wanderings*. New York: Dutton, 1962.

Steiner, Lina. "Apollon Grigor'ev's Theory of Russian Culture." *For Humanity's Sake: The Bildungsroman in Russian Culture*, 29–37. Toronto: University of Toronto Press, 2011.

Whittaker, Robert. "*My Literary and Moral Wanderings*: Apollon Grigor'ev and the Changing Cultural Topography of Moscow." *Slavic Review* 43, no. 3 (Fall 1983): 390–407.

Whittaker, Robert. *Russia's Last Romantic: Apollon Grigoryev (1822–64)*, 9–29. Lewiston, ME: Edwin Mellon Press, 1999.